EASY PIANO   4TH EDITION

BEST OF TODAY'S MOVIE HITS

ISBN 978-1-5400-8898-7

Characters and Artwork © Disney
Disney/Pixar elements © Disney/Pixar

HAL•LEONARD®

Visit Hal Leonard Online at
www.halleonard.com

Contact us:
Hal Leonard
7777 West Bluemound Road
Milwaukee, WI 53213
Email: info@halleonard.com

In Europe, contact:
Hal Leonard Europe Limited
42 Wigmore Street
Marylebone, London, W1U 2RN
Email: info@halleonardeurope.com

In Australia, contact:
Hal Leonard Australia Pty. Ltd.
4 Lentara Court
Cheltenham, Victoria, 3192 Australia
Email: info@halleonard.com.au

CONTENTS

THE BALLAD OF THE
LONESOME COWBOY

from TOY STORY 4

Music and Lyrics by
RANDY NEWMAN

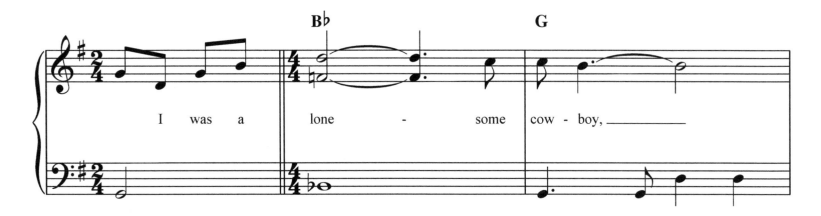

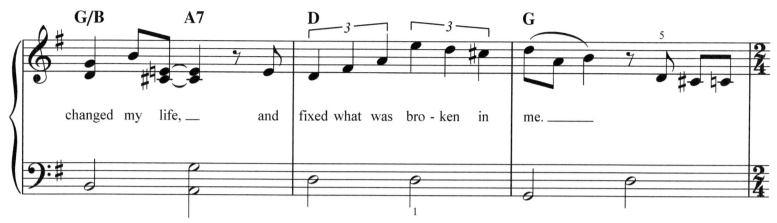

changed my life, ___ and fixed what was bro - ken in me. ___

I was a lone - some cow - boy, ___

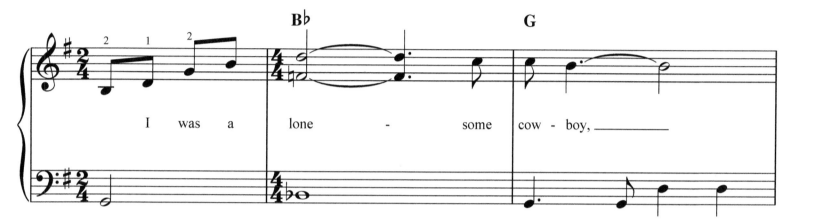

I did-n't have a friend. ___ Now I got friends com-in'

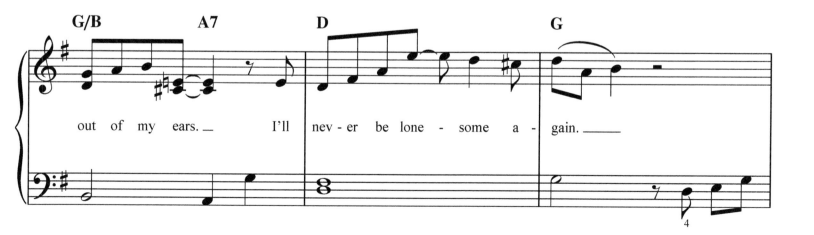

out of my ears. ___ I'll nev - er be lone - some a - gain. ___

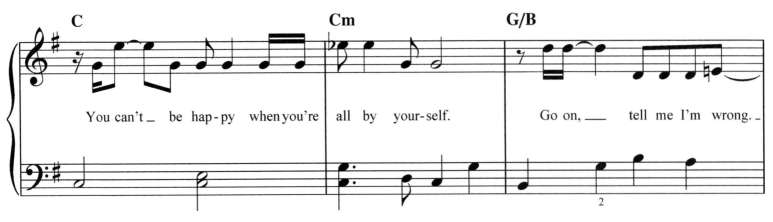

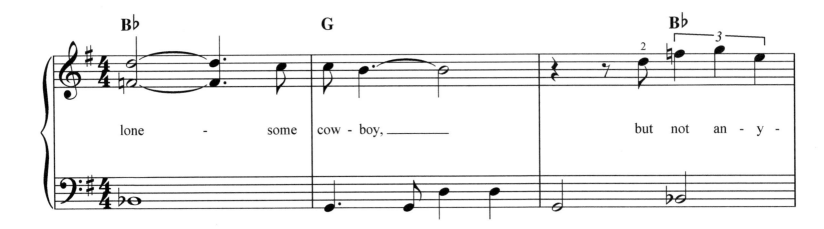

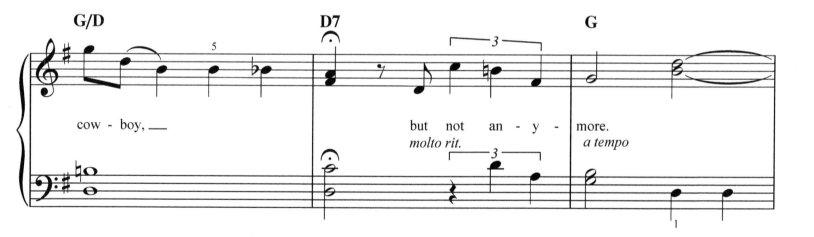

BEAUTIFUL GHOSTS

from the film CATS

Words and Music by TAYLOR SWIFT
and ANDREW LLOYD WEBBER

watch from the dark, wait for my life to start, with no beau - ty in my mem - o -
call them my friends and be bro - ken a - gain. Is this hope just a mys - ti - cal

ry.
dream?

All that I

want - ed

mf

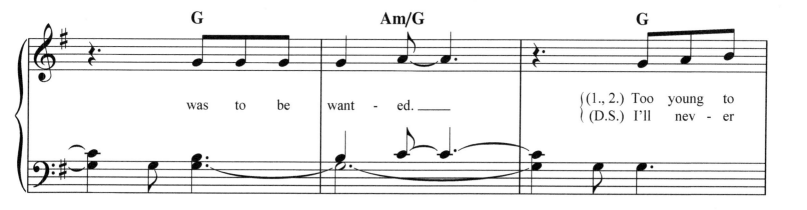

was to be want - ed.

((1., 2.) Too young to
((D.S.) I'll nev - er

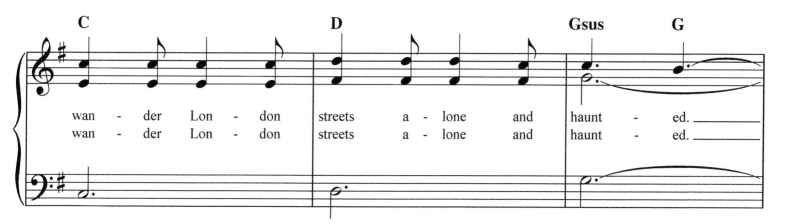

wan - der Lon - don streets a - lone and haunt - ed.
wan - der Lon - don streets a - lone and haunt - ed.

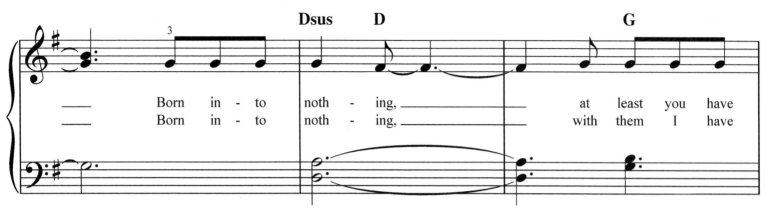

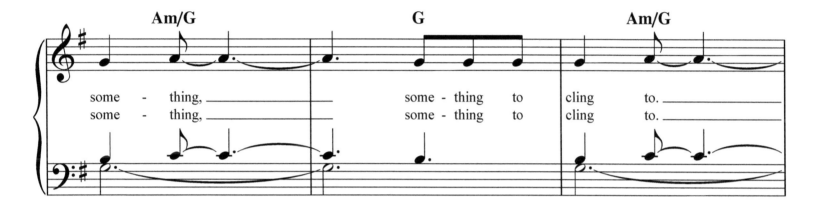

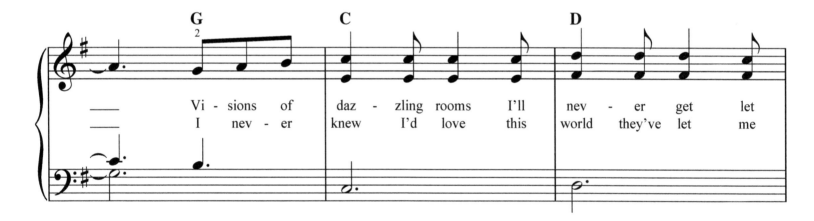

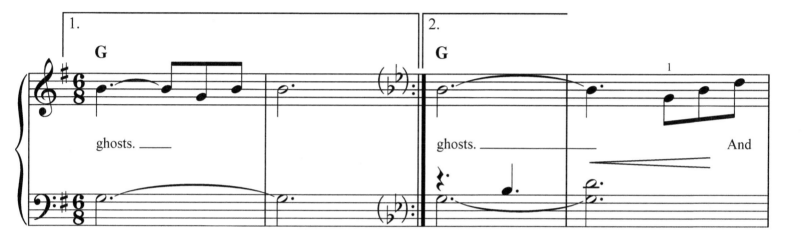

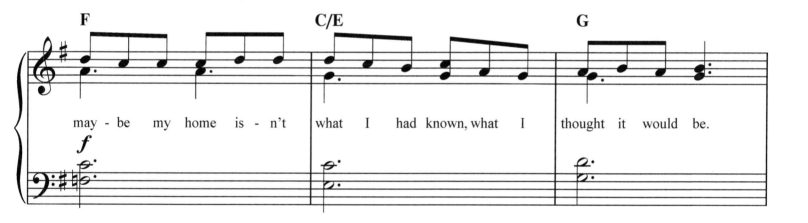

know that this life is - n't   safe, but it's wild and it's   free.

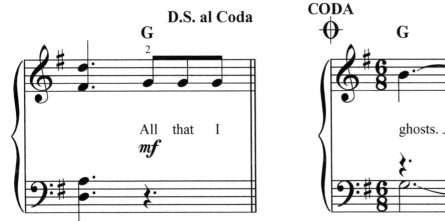

D.S. al Coda

All that I
mf

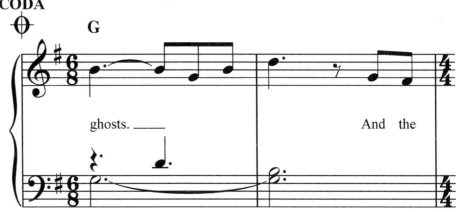

CODA

ghosts. _____   And the

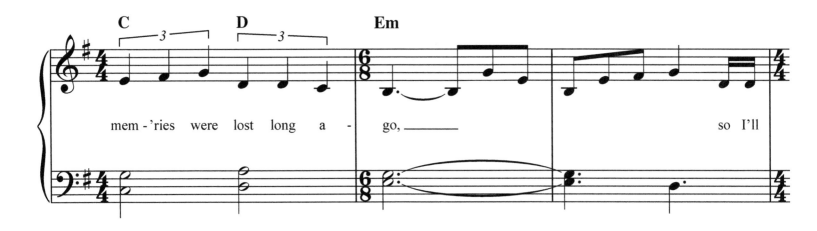

mem -'ries were lost long a - go, _____   so I'll

dance with these beau - ti - ful   ghosts. _____
rit.   *rit.*
f *a tempo*

CRAZY LITTLE THING CALLED LOVE

featured in BOHEMIAN RHAPSODY

Words and Music by
FREDDIE MERCURY

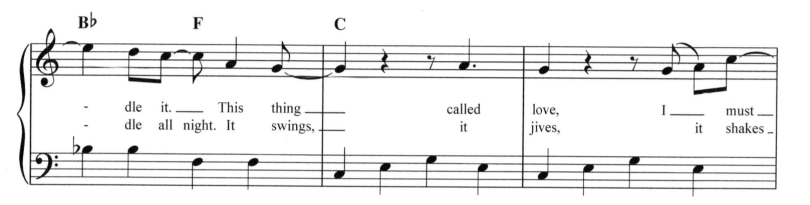

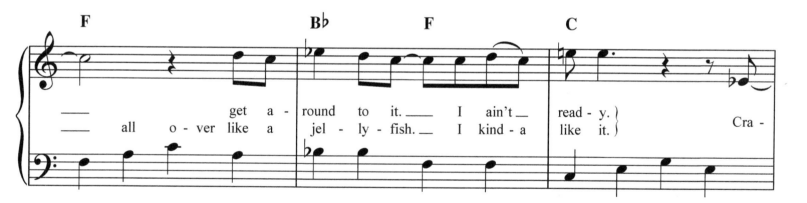

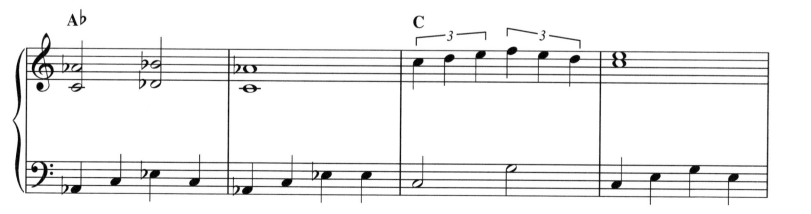

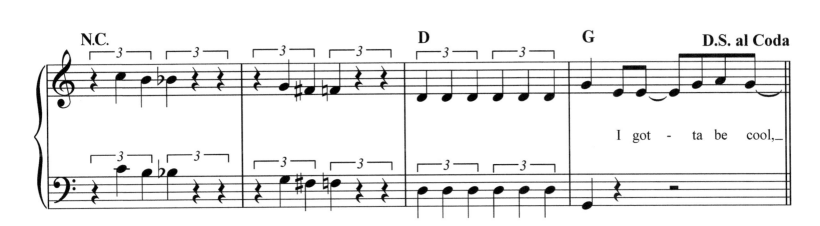

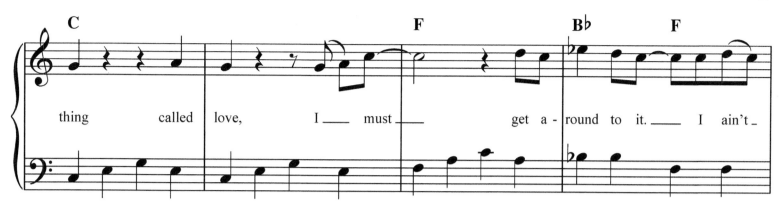

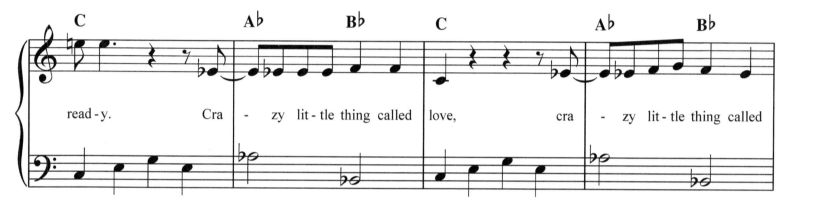

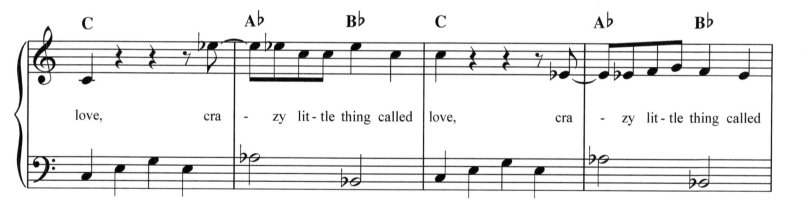

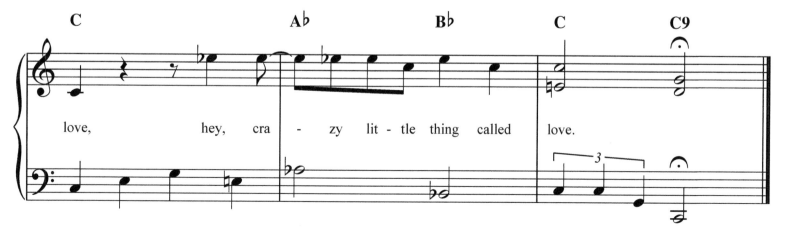

BUSY DOING NOTHING
from CHRISTOPHER ROBIN

Music and Lyrics by
RICHARD M. SHERMAN

Moderately, with a bounce

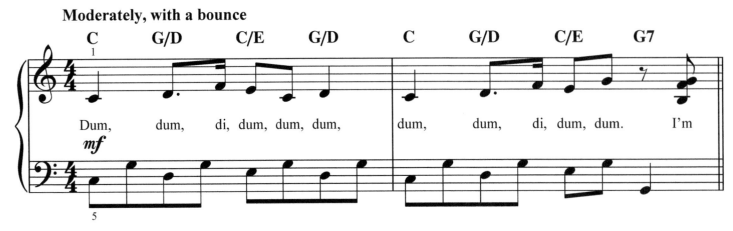

Dum, dum, di, dum, dum, dum, dum, dum, di, dum, dum. I'm

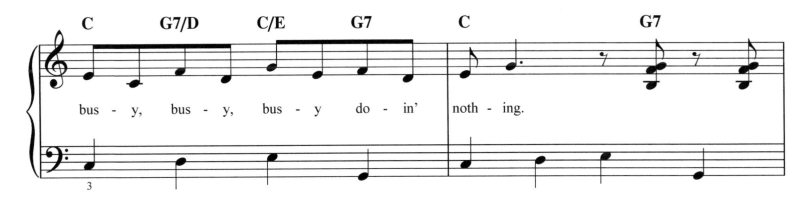

bus - y, bus - y, bus - y do - in' noth - ing.

Do - ing noth - ing, that's the life for me. For

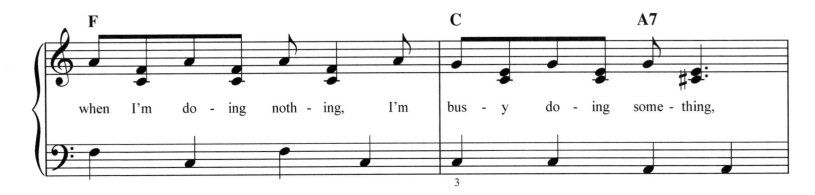

when I'm do - ing noth - ing, I'm bus - y do - ing some - thing,

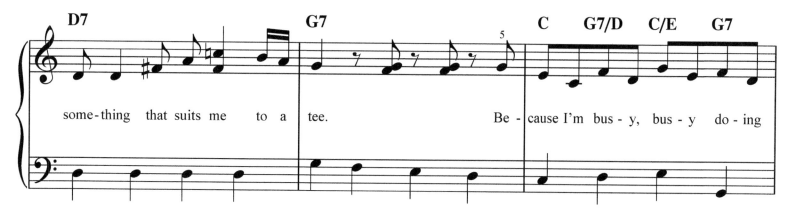

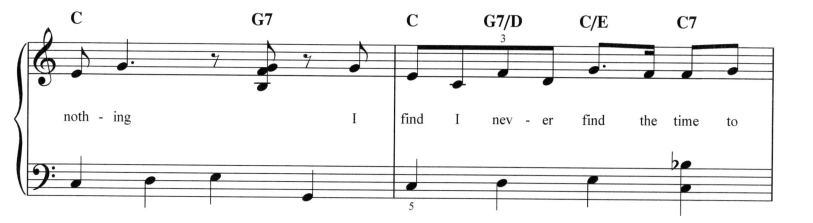

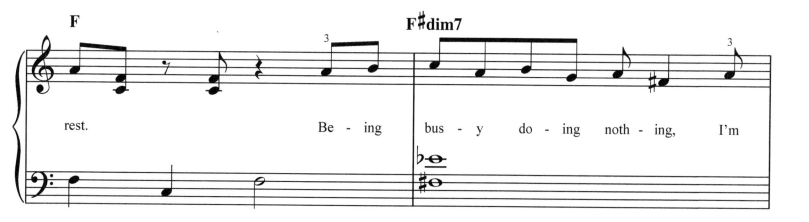

CARRY ON

featured in POKÉMON: DETECTIVE PIKACHU

Words and Music by KYRRE GORVELL-DAHLL,
JOSHUA CUMBEE, AFSHIN SALMANI,
ILAN KIDRON, NATALIE DUNN
and RITA ORA

Moderately fast

Walk-ing a-lone and the shores are long - ing, ___
Talk to the wind on the o - pen o - cean, ___

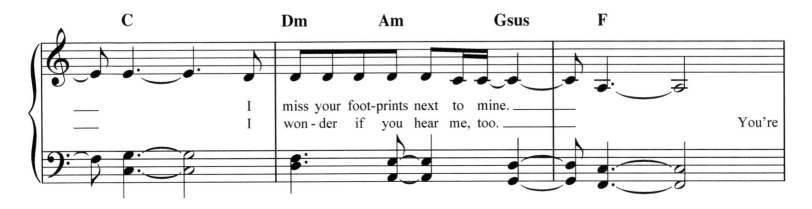

I miss your foot-prints next to mine. ___
I won-der if you hear me, too. ___
You're

Sure as the waves on the sand are wash - ing, ___
wrapped in my arms with ___ ev - 'ry mo - ment, ___
the

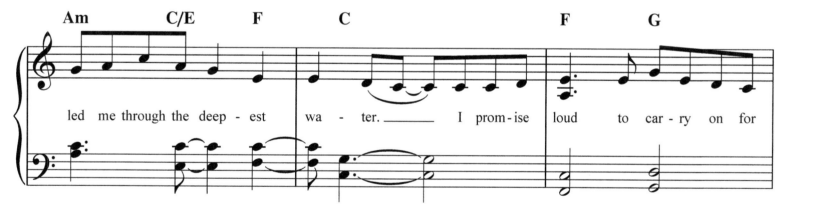

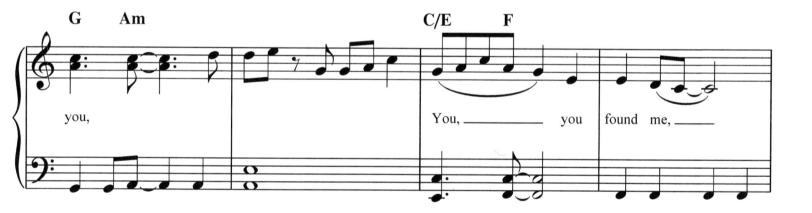

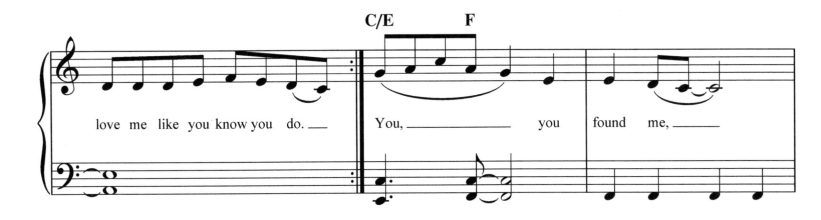

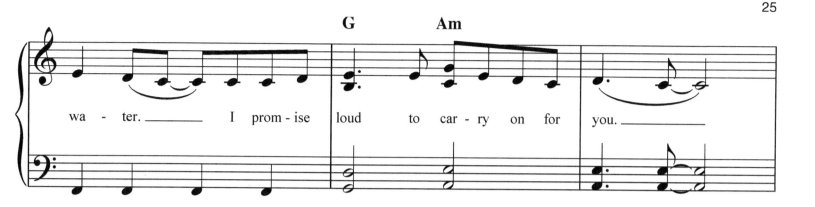

DOWNTON ABBEY

(Theme)
from DOWNTON ABBEY

Music by JOHN LUNN

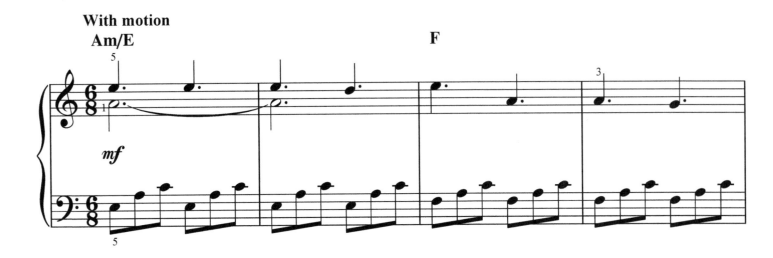

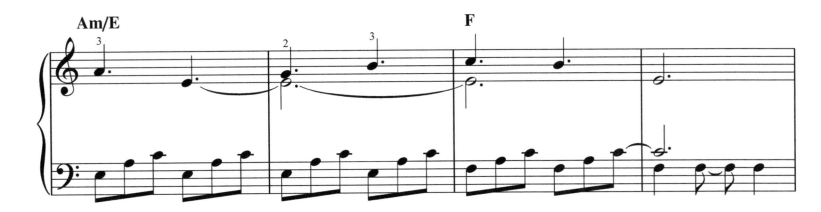

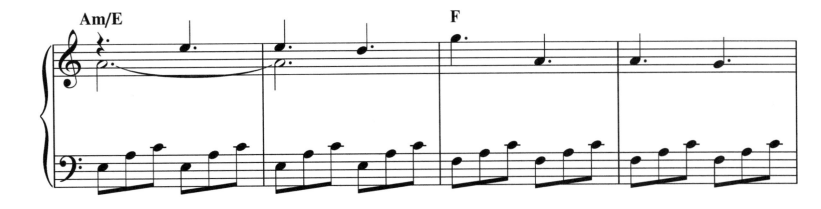

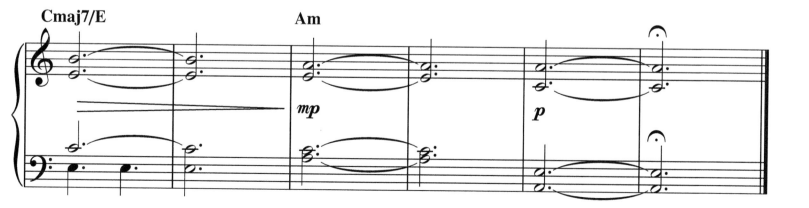

ELASTIGIRL IS BACK

from INCREDIBLES 2

Composed by MICHAEL GIACCHINO

Moderately fast

SHALLOW
from A STAR IS BORN

Words and Music by STEFANI GERMANOTTA,
MARK RONSON, ANDREW WYATT
and ANTHONY ROSSOMANDO

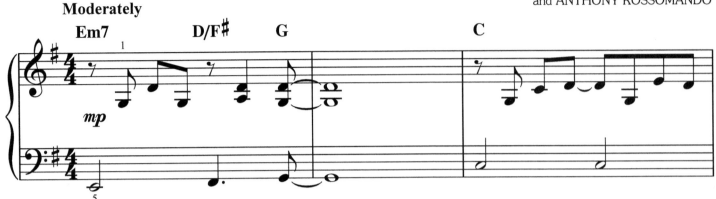

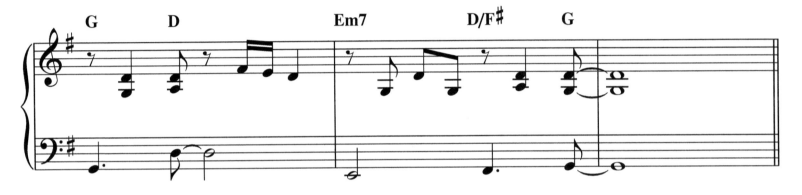

Tell me some-thing, girl: ____ are you hap-py in this
Tell me some-thing, boy: ____ aren't you tired, __ tryin' to

mod-ern world, __ or do you need more? __
fill that void, __ or do you need more? __

31

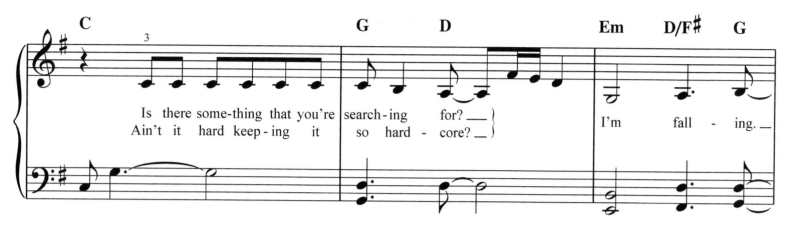

Is there some-thing that you're search-ing for? ⎫
Ain't it hard keep-ing it so hard - core? ⎭

I'm fall - ing.

In all the good times I find my - self long - ing

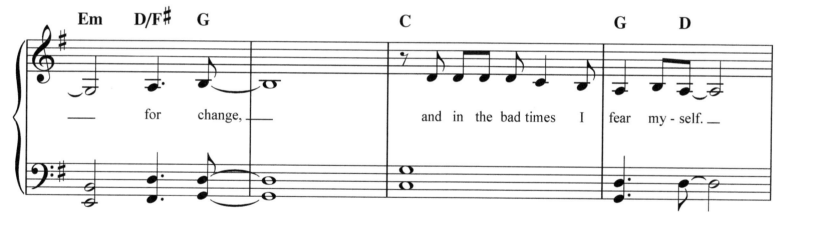

for change, and in the bad times I fear my - self.

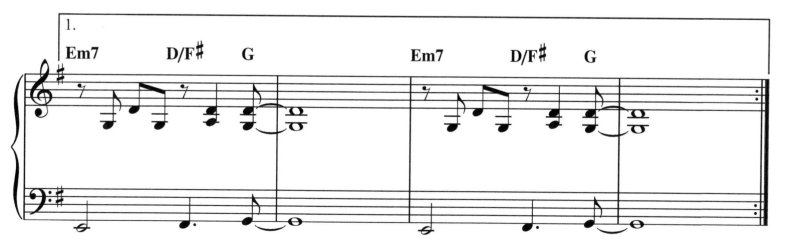

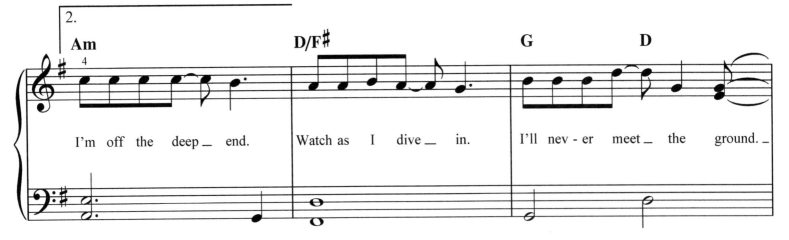

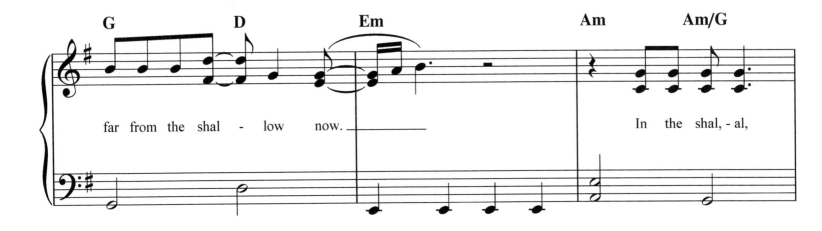

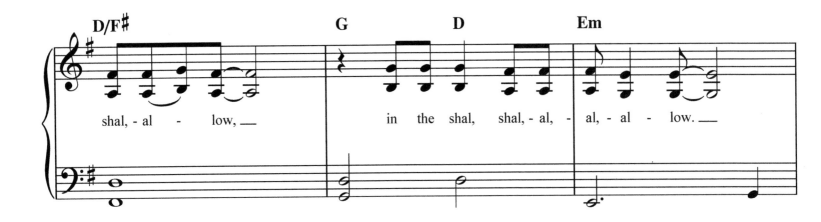

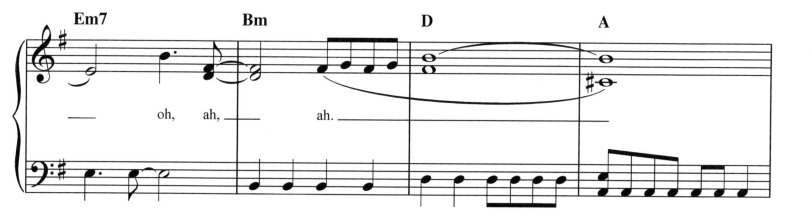

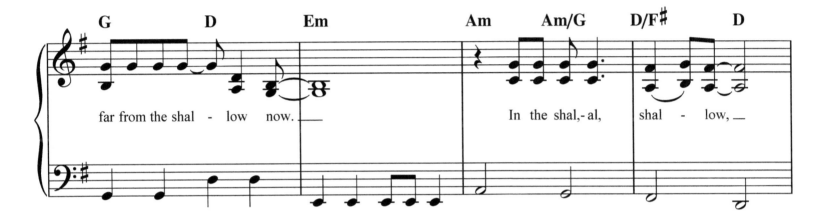

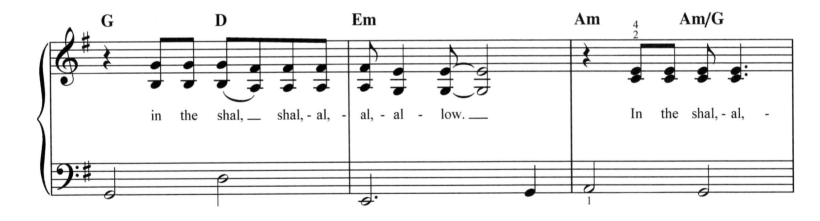

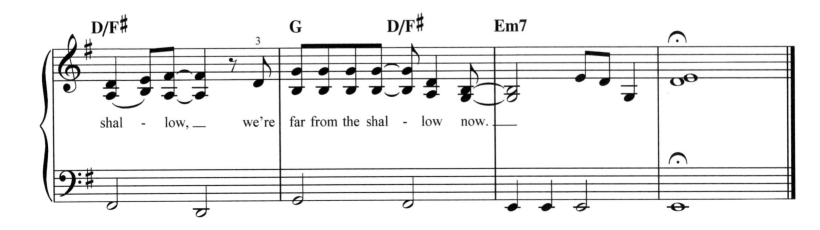

THE HIDDEN WORLD
from the Motion Picture HOW TO TRAIN YOUR DRAGON: THE HIDDEN WORLD

By JOHN POWELL

Slowly

Broaden

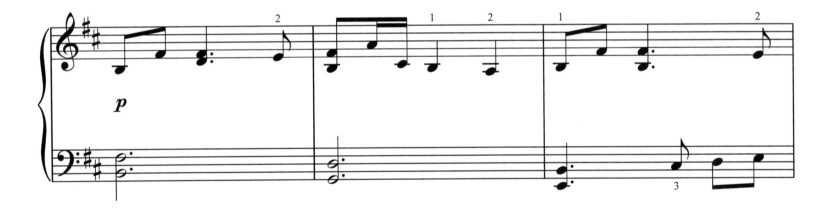

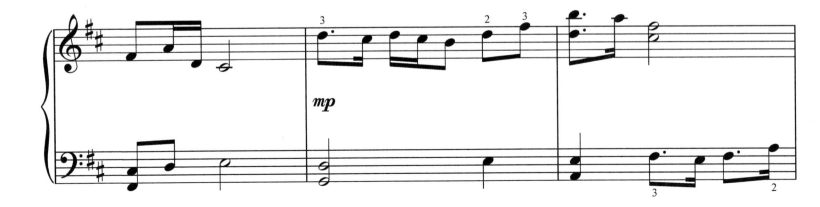

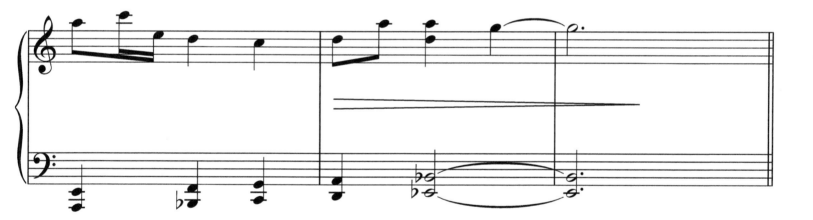

SPIRIT
from Disney's THE LION KING 2019

Written by TIMOTHY McKENZIE,
ILYA SALMANZADEH and BEYONCÉ

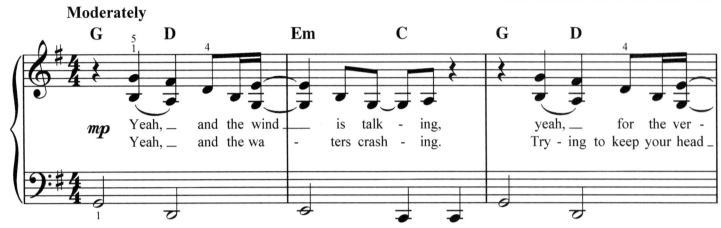

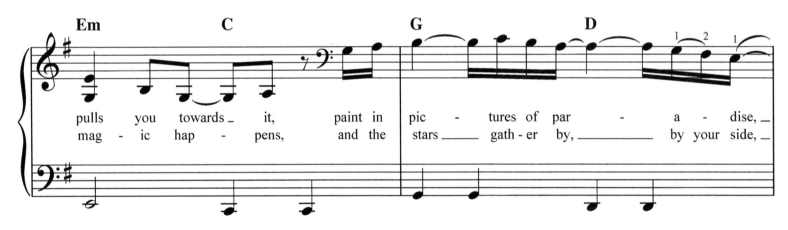

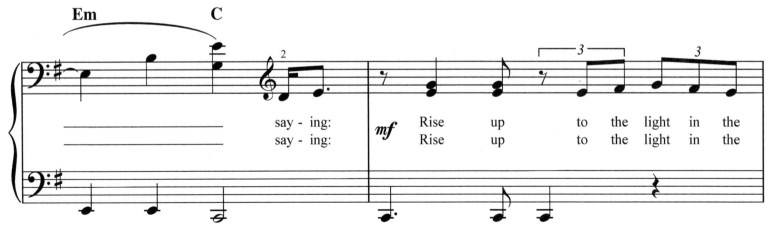

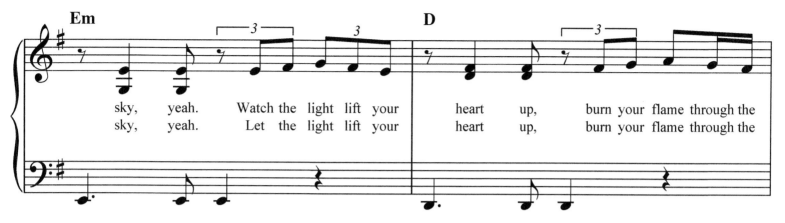

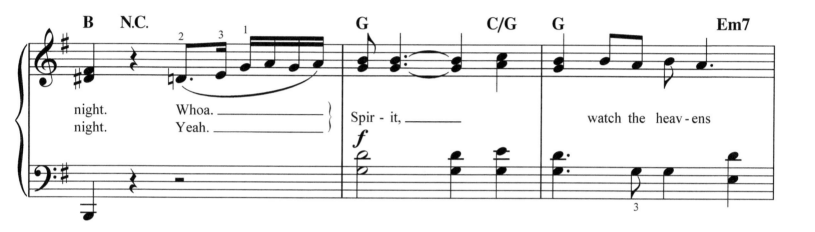

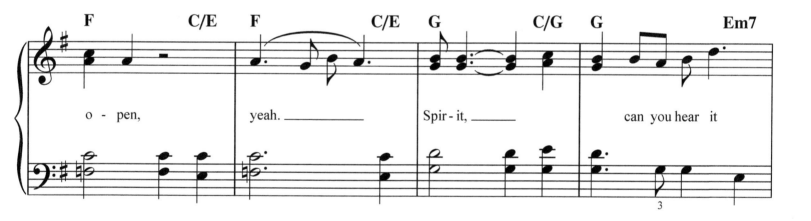

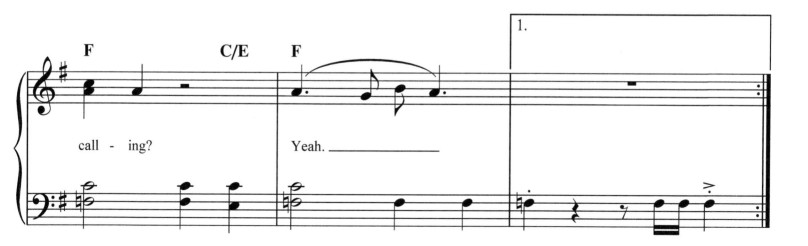

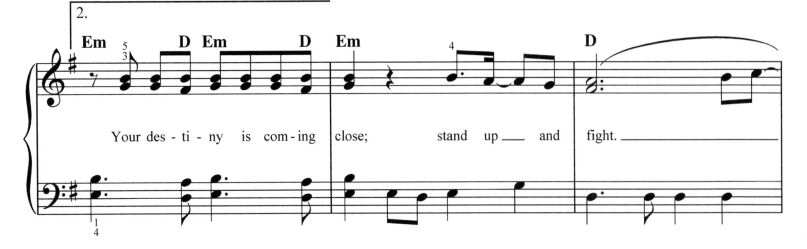

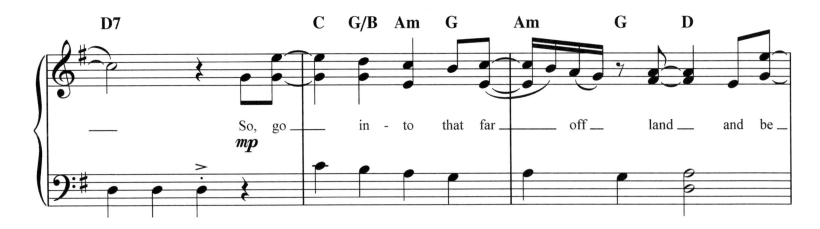

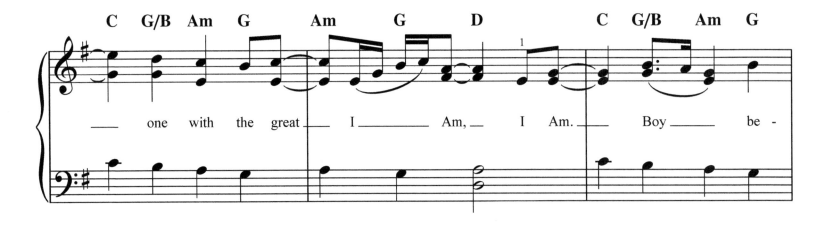

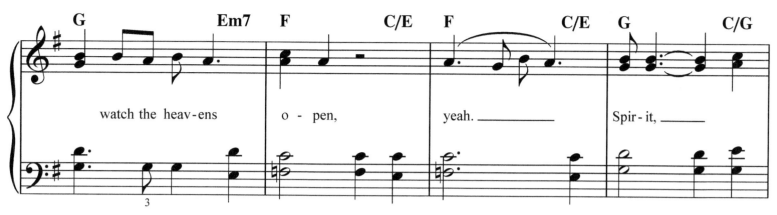

watch the heav-ens   o - pen,   yeah. _____   Spir- it, _____

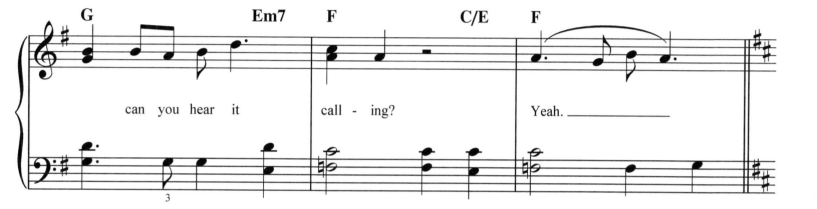

can you hear it   call - ing?   Yeah. _____

Spir - it, _____   watch the heav - ens   o - pen,

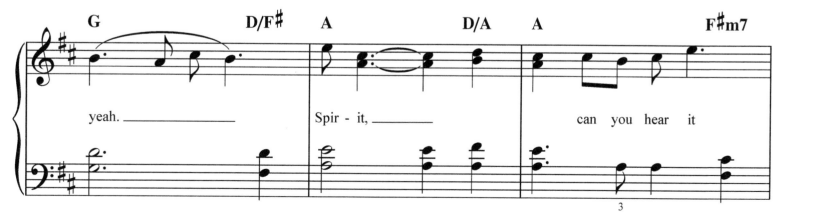

yeah. _____   Spir - it, _____   can you hear it

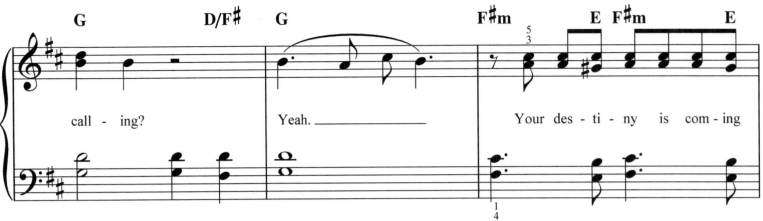

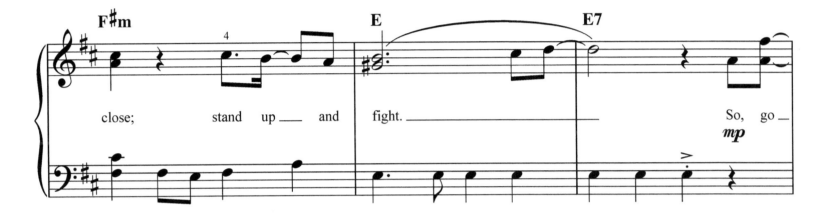

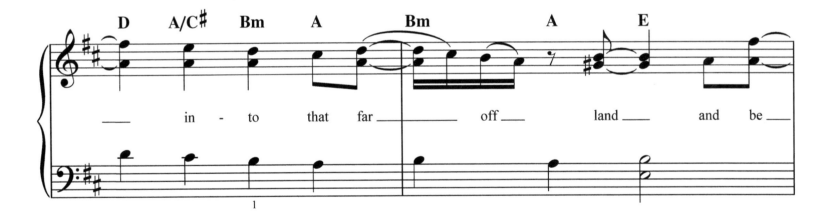

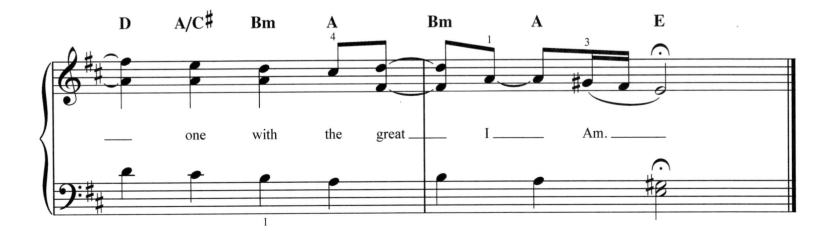

HIDEAWAY
from the film WONDER PARK

Words and Music by JONNY SHORR,
KATIE STUMP, WILLIAM BEHLENDORF
and EMILY KOCONTES

Moderately

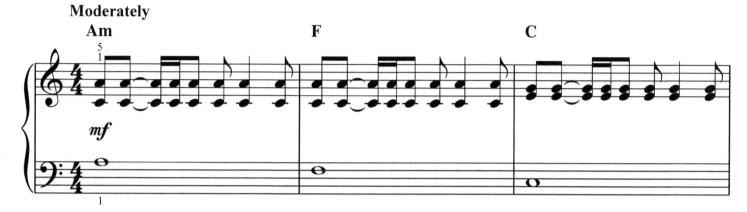

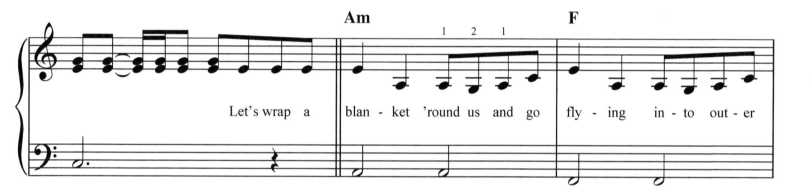

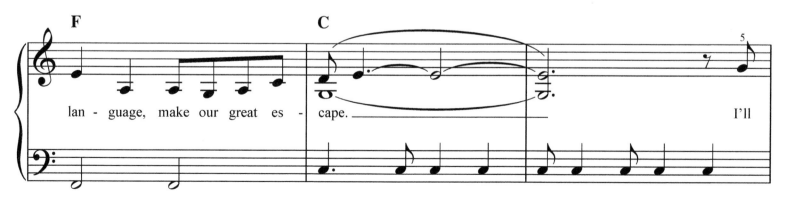

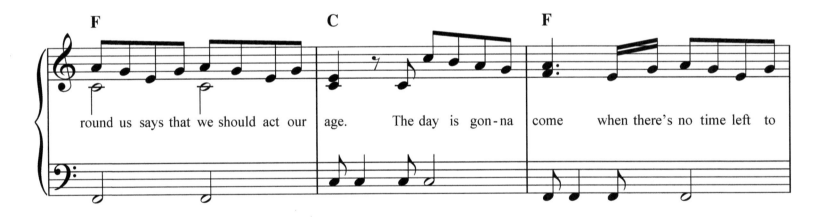

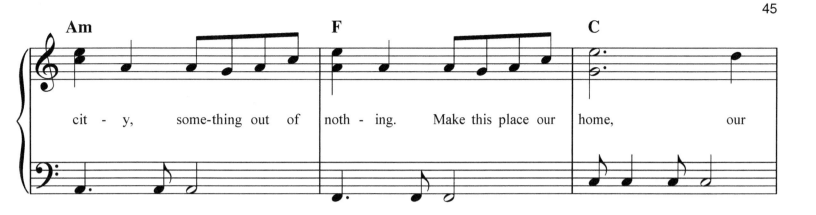

cit - y, some-thing out of noth - ing. Make this place our home, our

home. Stay make - be - liev - ing, we'll go dis - ap - pear - ing. Who would ev - er

know? We'll nev - er be too far __ a - part 'cause

D.S. al Coda

in the end, you and I both know there's some - where we can go. So, let's just play pre -

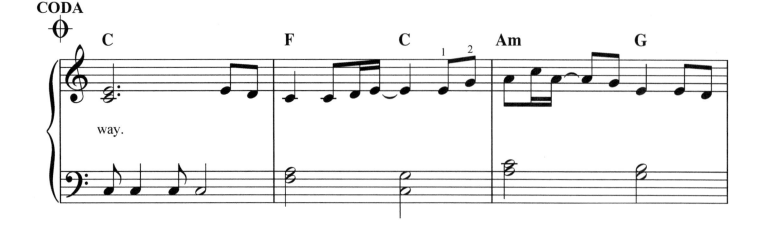

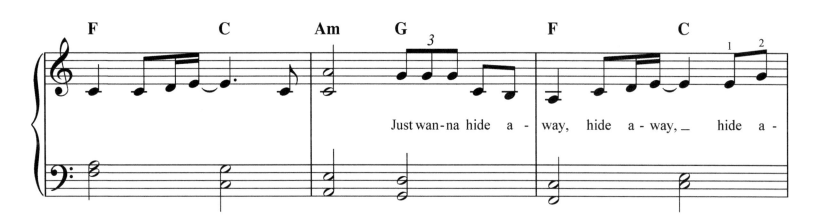

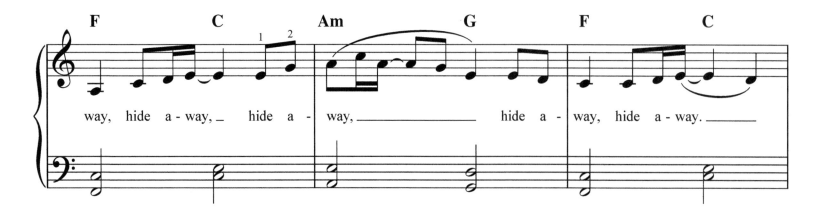

So, let's just play pre - tend and find a se - cret place when the world a -

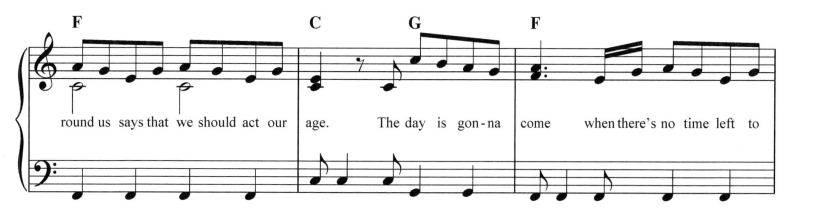

round us says that we should act our age. The day is gon-na come when there's no time left to

waste, _____ but we'll nev - er grow up. I say we hide a -

1.
way. So, let's just play pre -

2.
way. Don't make me grow up. I say we hide a-way.

I BELIEVE
from A WRINKLE IN TIME

Words and Music by KHALED KHALED,
DEMI LOVATO, DENISIA ANDREWS
and BRITTANY CONEY

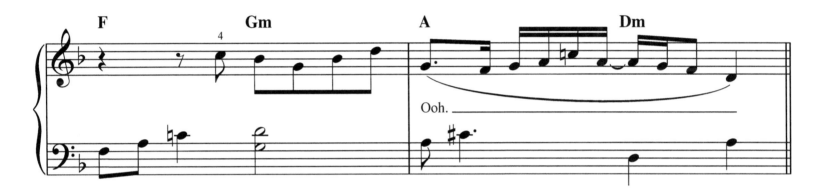

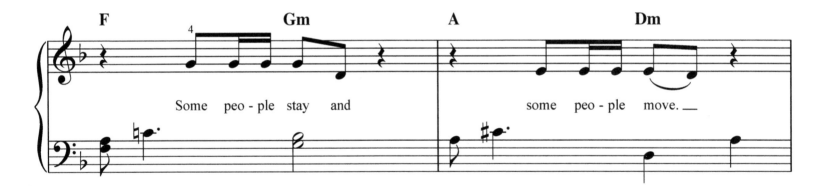

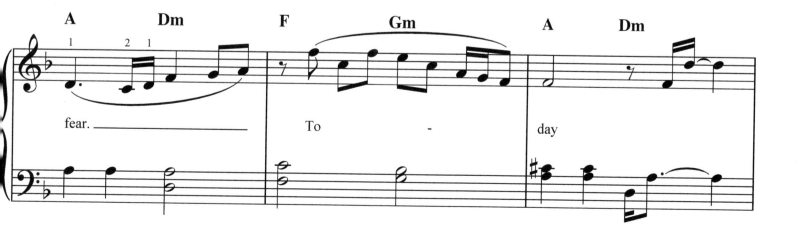

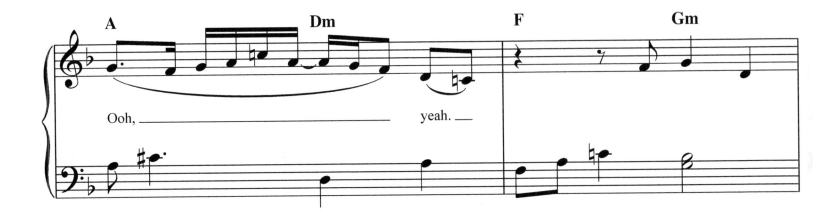

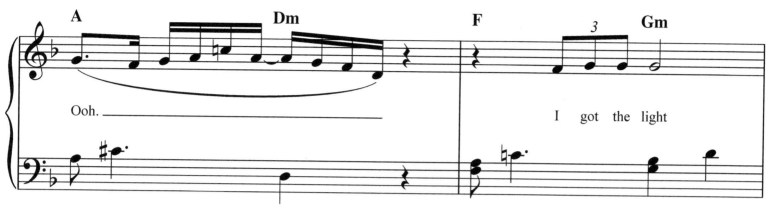

Ooh. _____

I got the light

in-side of me, __

and I've got no choice

but to let it breathe. _____

As long as there is love, __

I can make it an-y-where I go. __

If I fol-low my dreams, I'll end up build-ing a yel-low brick road. __

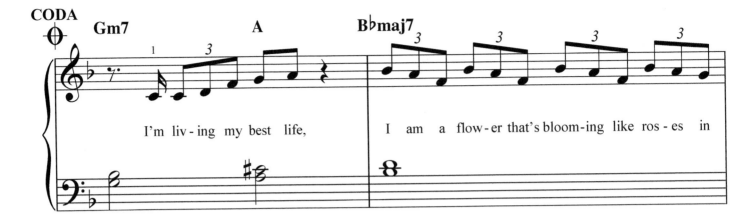

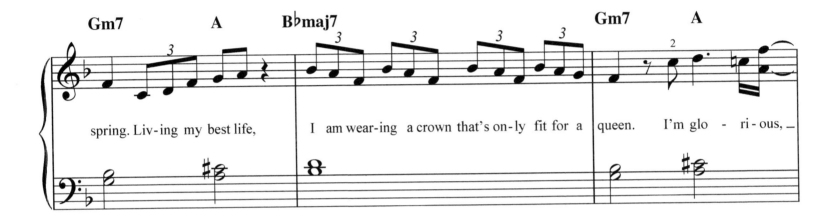

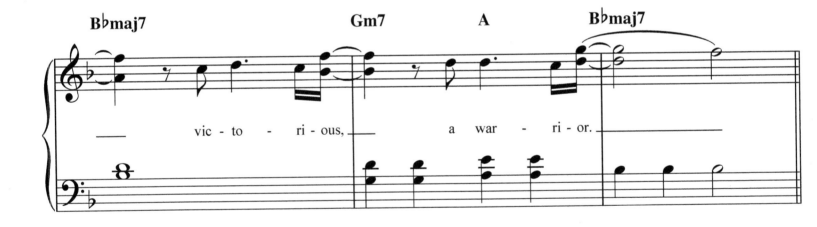

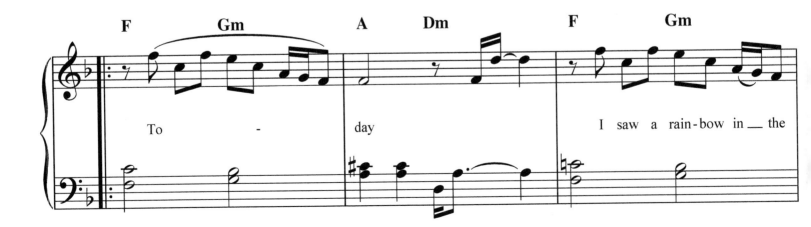

rain.

It told me I can do _____ an - y - thing _ if I be-

lieve, I be-lieve, I be-lieve in me. I be- lieve, I be-lieve, I be-lieve in me.

1.

When times got hard, I went

hard- er.

Best thing I ev - er did _ was be-lieve _ in me.

I be - lieve.

2.

To succeed, you must believe.

(We the best music.)

I believe. (Another one.)

A wrinkle in time.

rit.

A MILLION DREAMS

from THE GREATEST SHOWMAN

Words and Music by BENJ PASEK
and JUSTIN PAUL

Moderately, with intensity

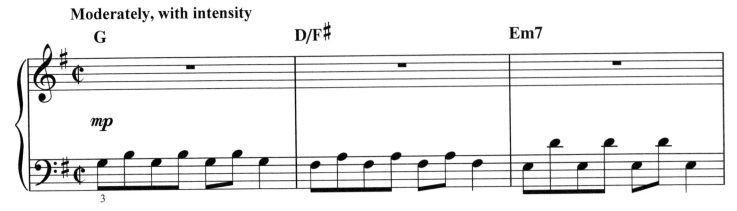

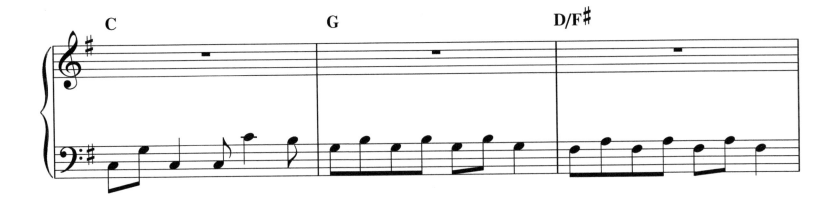

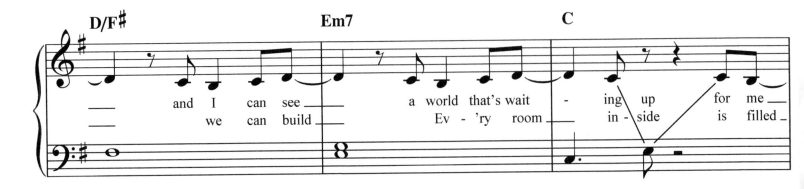

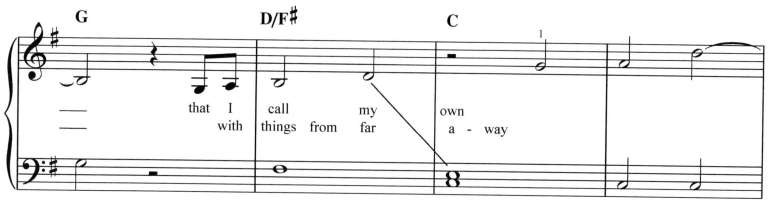

that I call my own
with things from my far a - way

Through the dark, through the door, through where no
Spe - cial things I com - pile, each one there

one's been be - fore, but it feels like home
to make you smile on a rain - y day

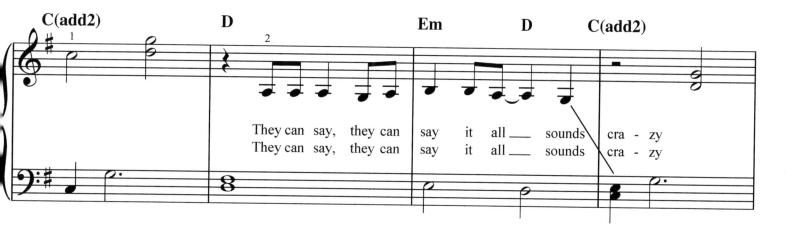

They can say, they can say it all sounds cra - zy
They can say, they can say it all sounds cra - zy

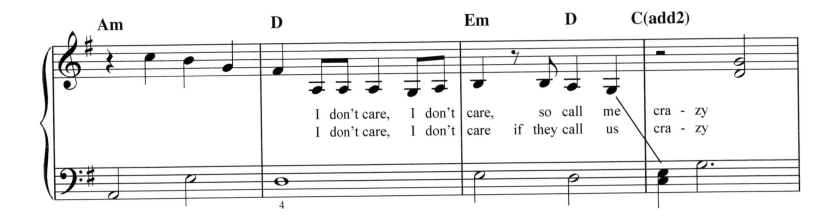

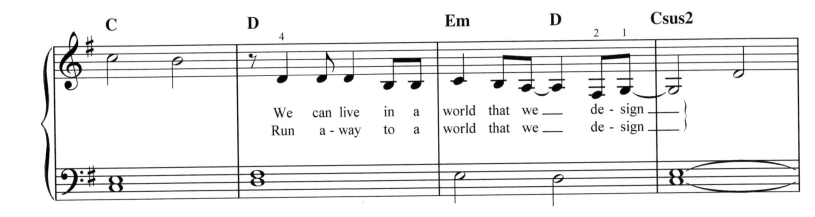

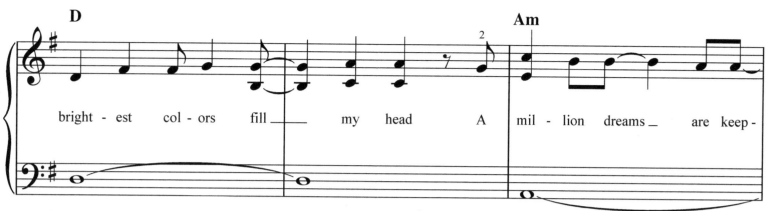

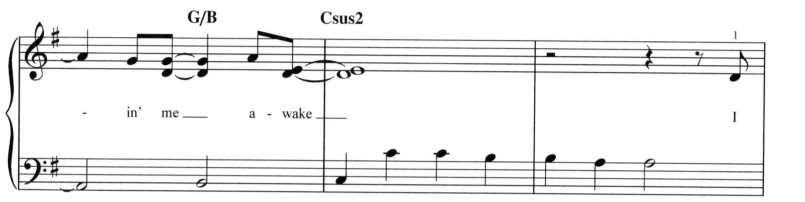

58

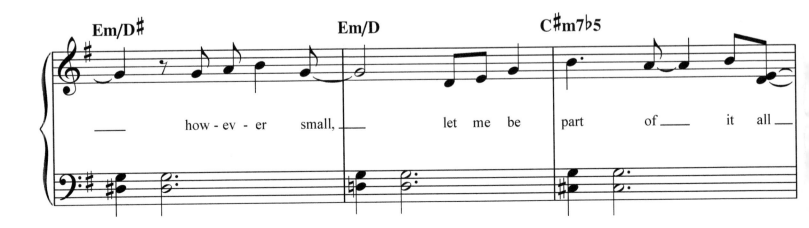

59

'Cause ev - 'ry night __ I lie __ in bed __ the

bright - est col - ors fill __ my head A mil - lion dreams __ are keep -

- in' me __ a - wake __ A mil - lion dreams, a mil - lion dreams __ I

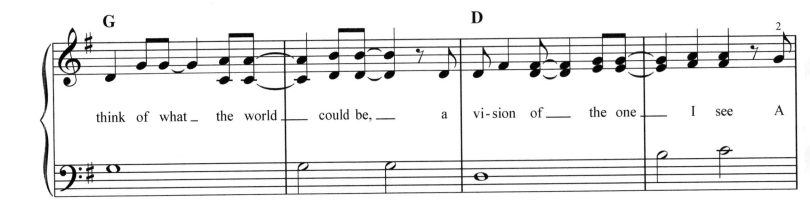

think of what __ the world __ could be, __ a vi - sion of __ the one __ I see A

mil - lion dreams __ is all __ it's gon - na take __

A mil - lion dreams __ for the world we're gon - na make __

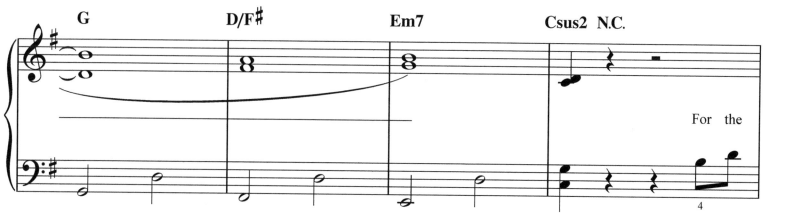

For the

world we're gon - na make

THE PLACE WHERE LOST THINGS GO

from MARY POPPINS RETURNS

Music by MARC SHAIMAN
Lyrics by SCOTT WITTMAN and MARC SHAIMAN

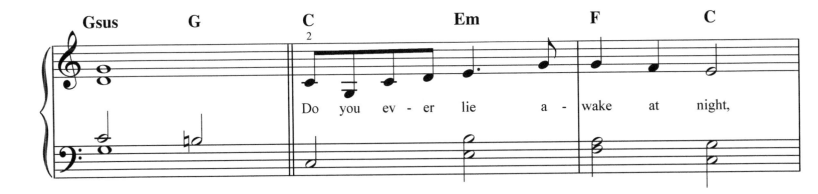

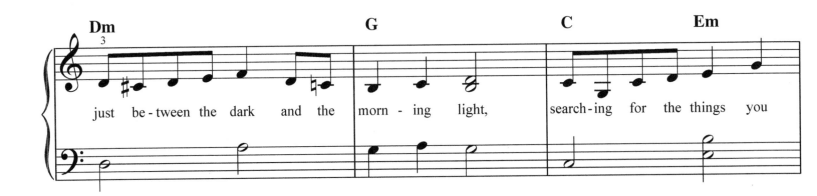

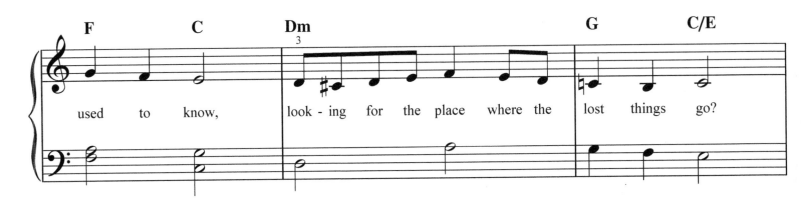

63

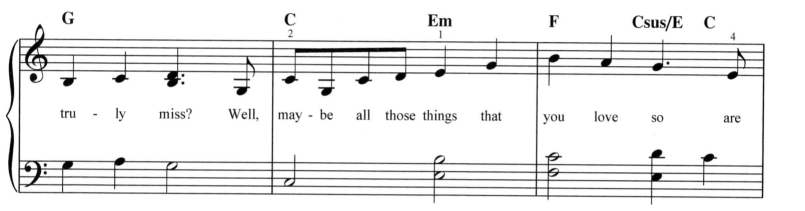

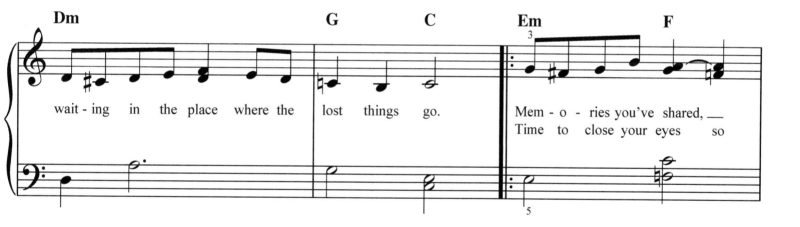

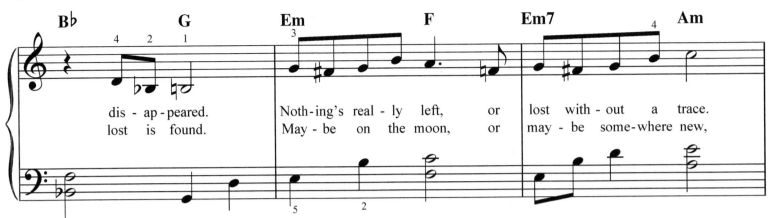

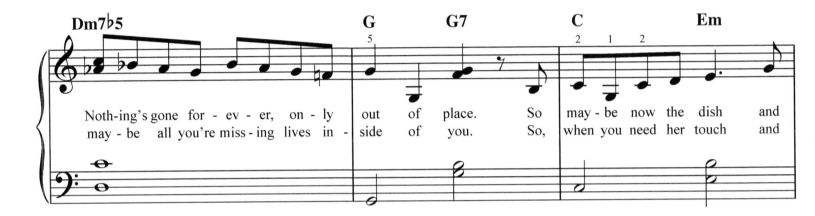

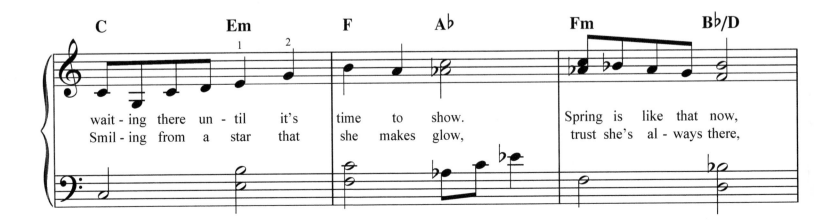

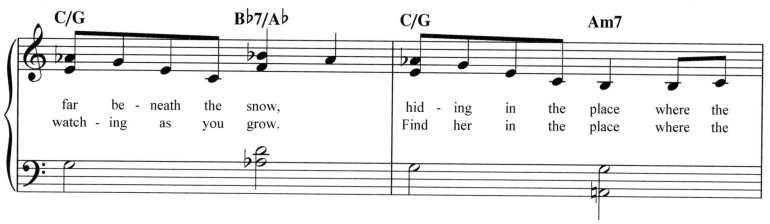

far be - neath the snow,
watch - ing as you grow.

hid - ing in the place where the
Find her in the place where the

lost things go.
lost things

poco rall.

a tempo

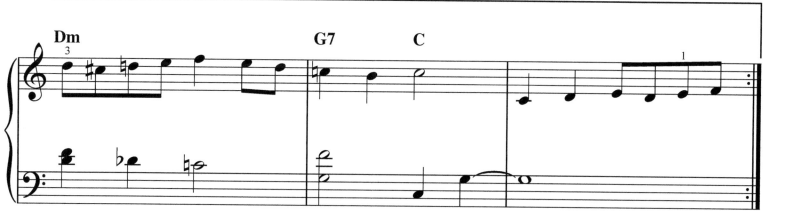

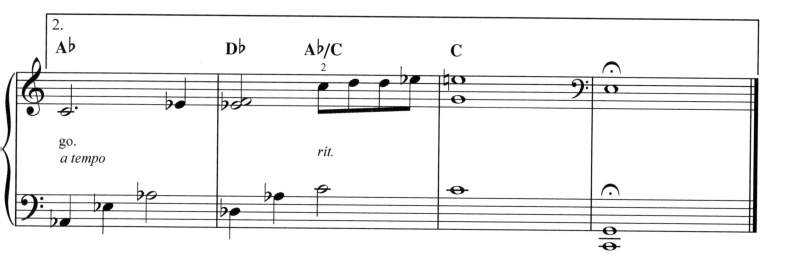

go.

a tempo

rit.

PROUD CORAZÓN

from COCO

Music by GERMAINE FRANCO
Lyrics by ADRIAN MOLINA

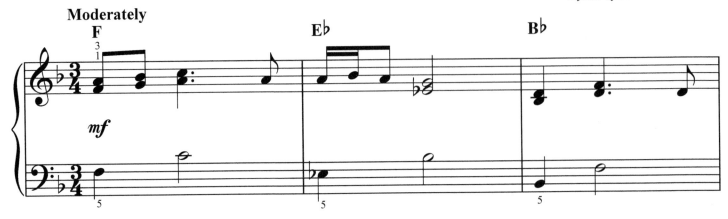

last night it seemed ___ that I dreamed a - bout

you.

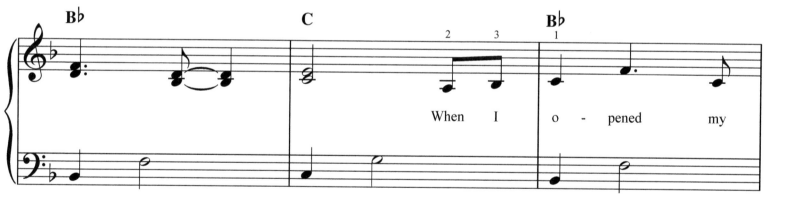

When I o - pened my

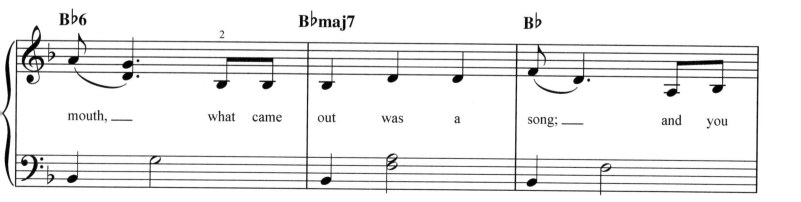

mouth, ___ what came out was a song; ___ and you

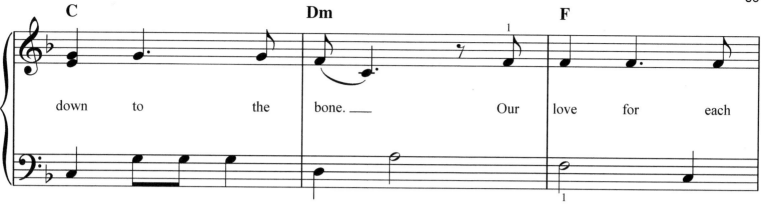

down to the bone. ___ Our love for each

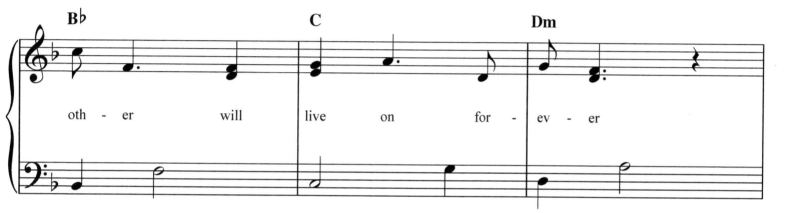

oth - er will live on for - ev - er

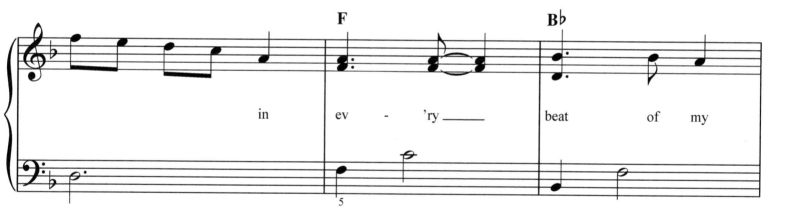

in ev - 'ry ___ beat of my

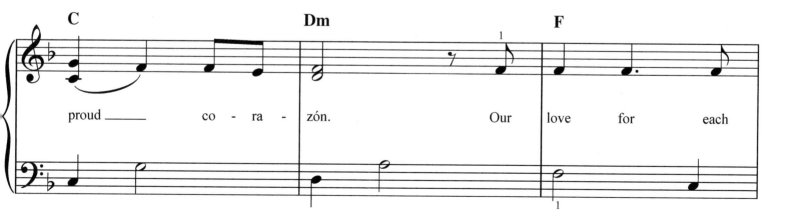

proud ___ co - ra - zón. Our love for each

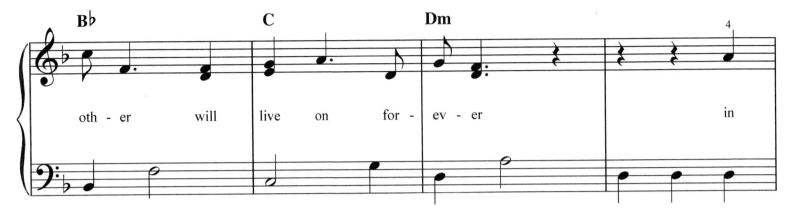

oth - er will live on for - ev - er in

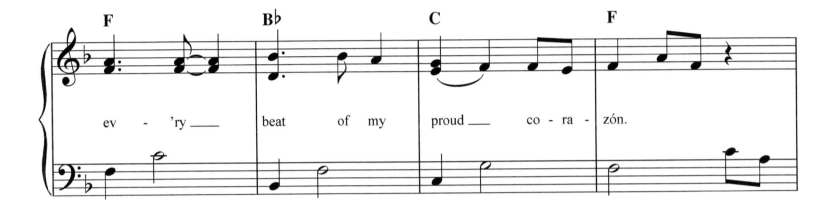

ev - 'ry ___ beat of my proud ___ co - ra - zón.

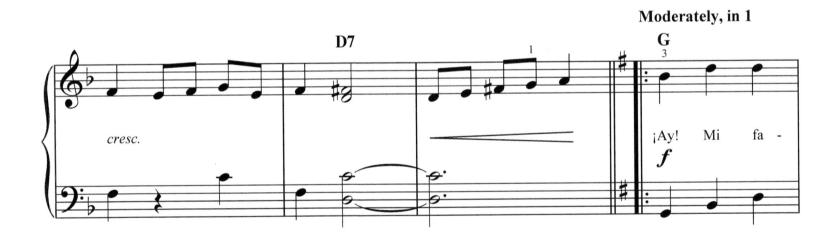

cresc.

Moderately, in 1

¡Ay! Mi fa -

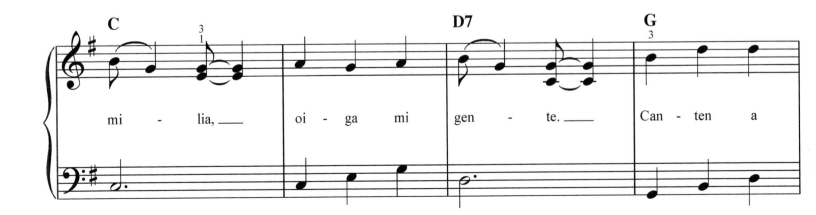

mi - lia, ___ oi - ga mi gen - te. ___ Can - ten a

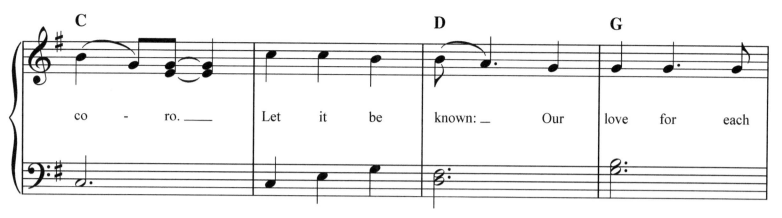

co - ro. ___ Let it be known: ___ Our love for each

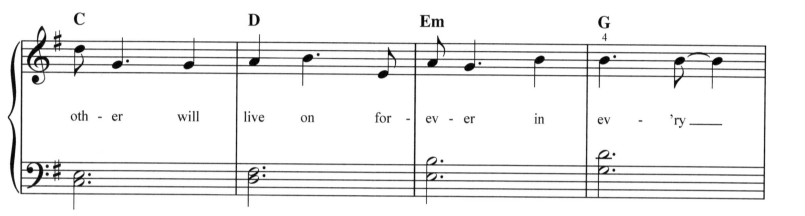

oth - er will live on for - ev - er in ev - 'ry ___

beat of my proud ___ co - ra - zón. proud ___ co - ra-

zón.

SPEECHLESS
from ALADDIN 2019

Music by ALAN MENKEN
Lyrics by BENJ PASEK and JUSTIN PAUL

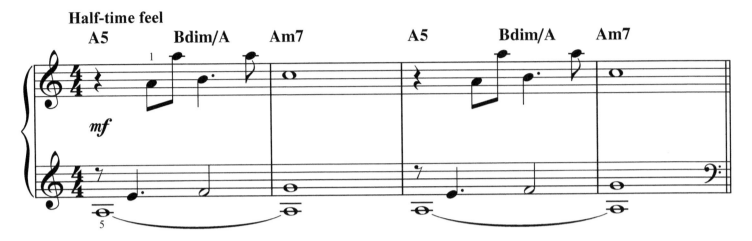

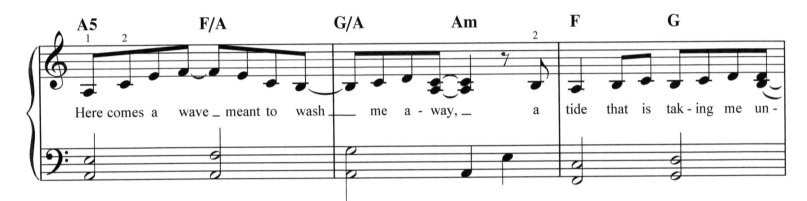

Here comes a wave meant to wash me a-way, a tide that is tak-ing me un-

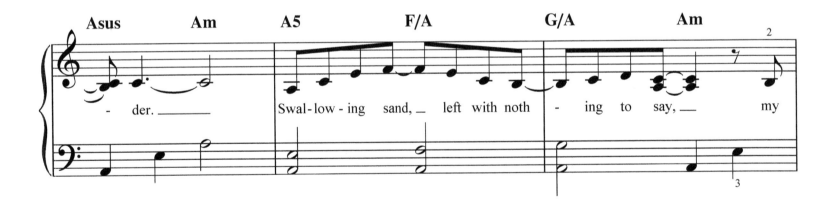

-der. Swal-low-ing sand, left with noth-ing to say, my

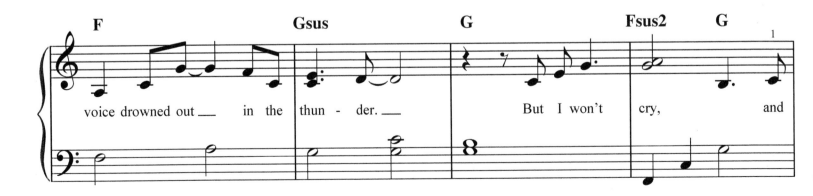

voice drowned out in the thun-der. But I won't cry, and

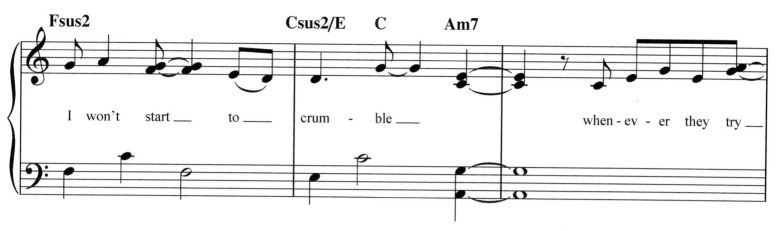

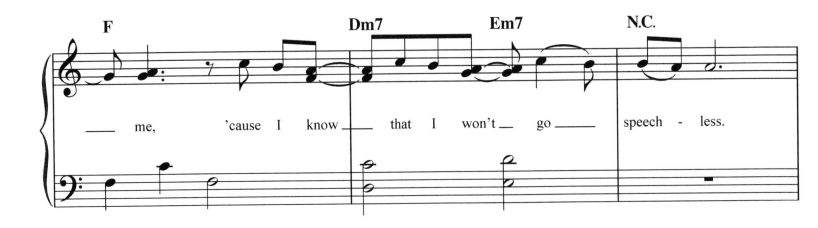

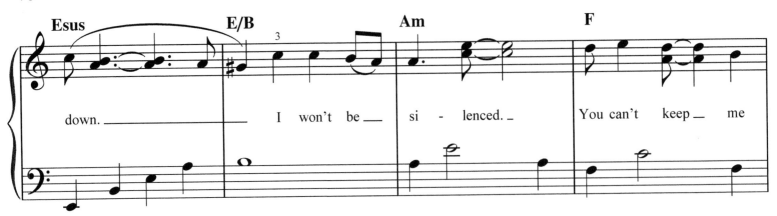

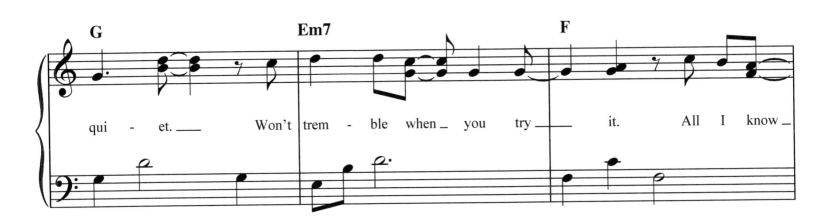

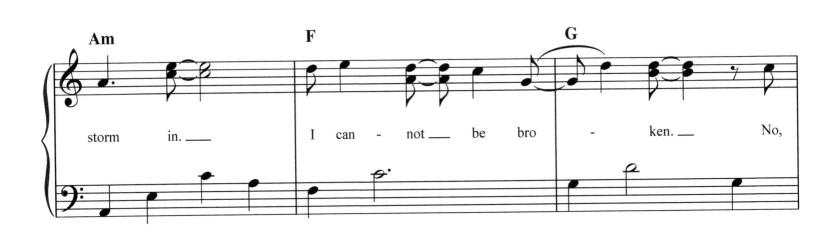

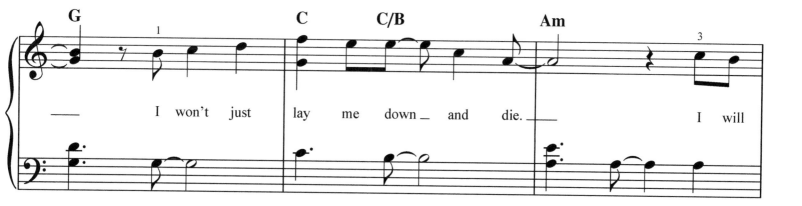

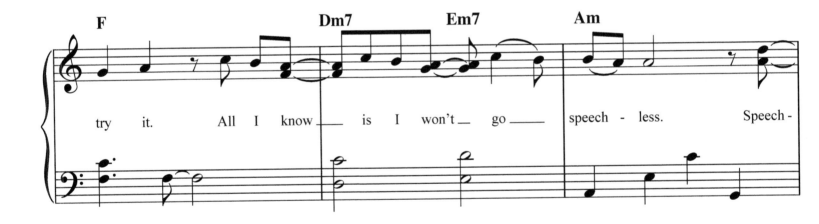

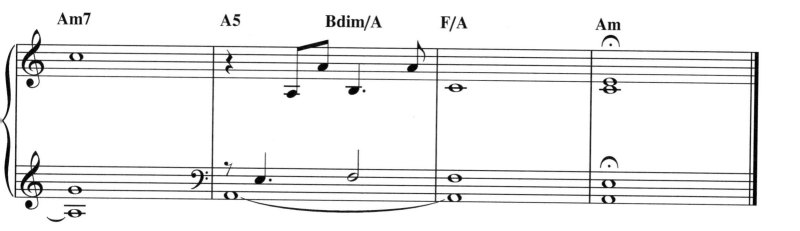

WON'T YOU BE MY NEIGHBOR?

(It's a Beautiful Day in the Neighborhood)
featured in A BEAUTIFUL DAY IN THE NEIGHBORHOOD

Words and Music by
FRED ROGERS

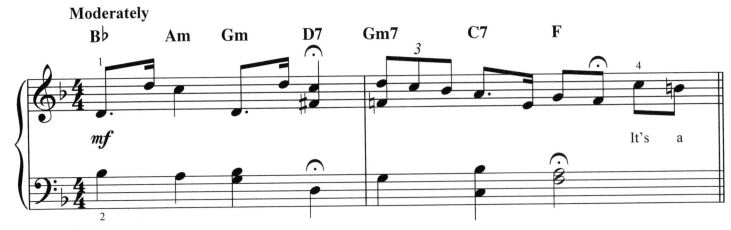

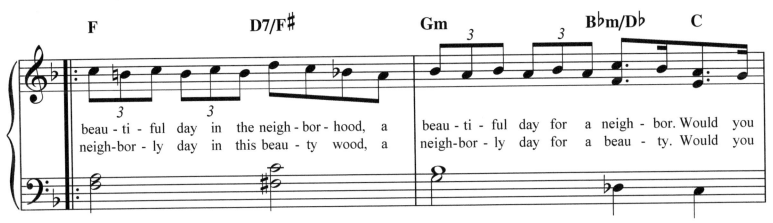

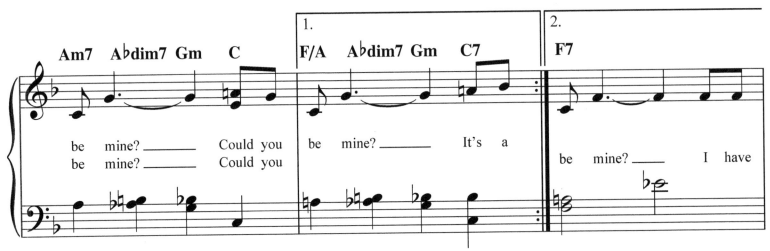

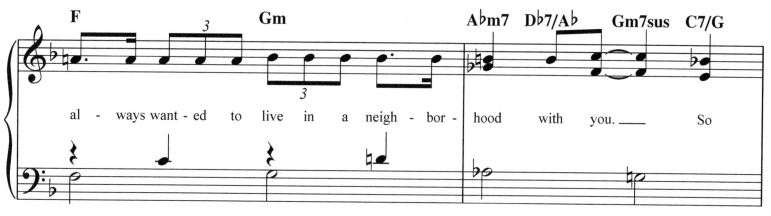

YESTERDAY
featured in YESTERDAY

Words and Music by JOHN LENNON
and PAUL McCARTNEY

Moderately, with expression

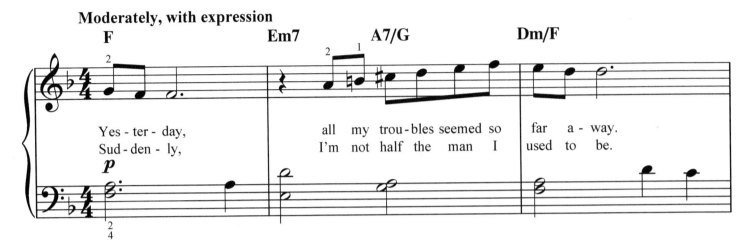

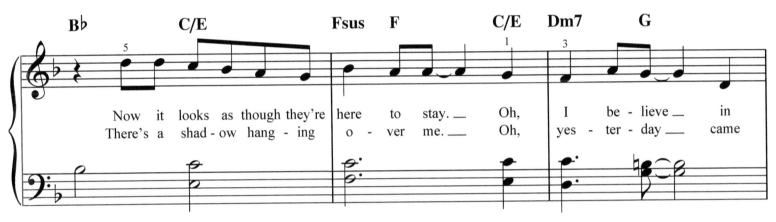

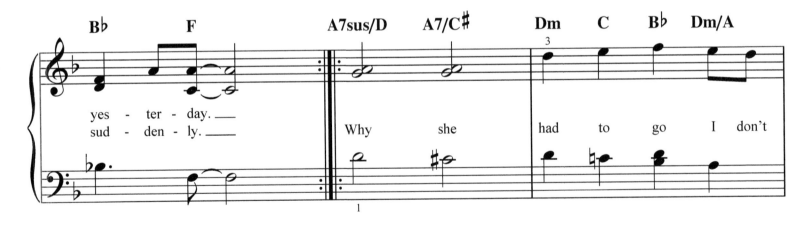

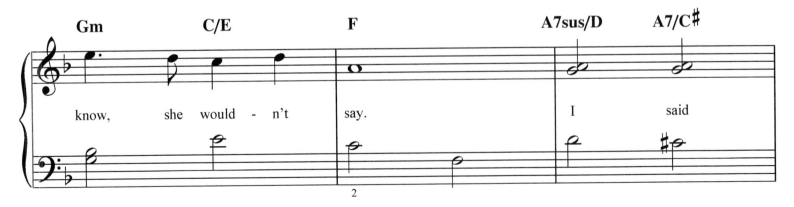

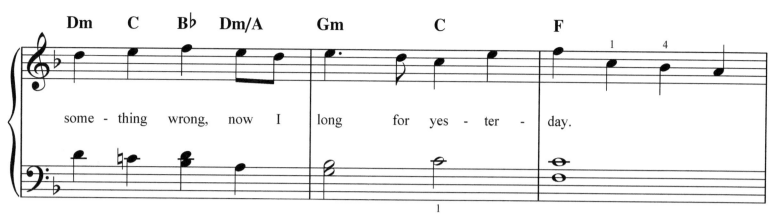

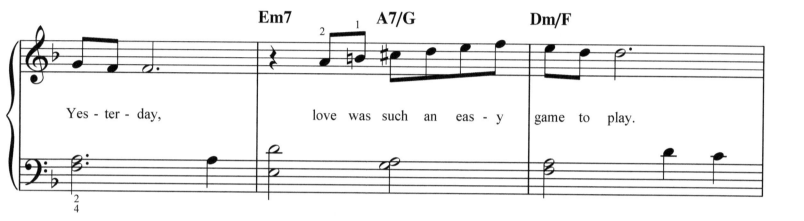

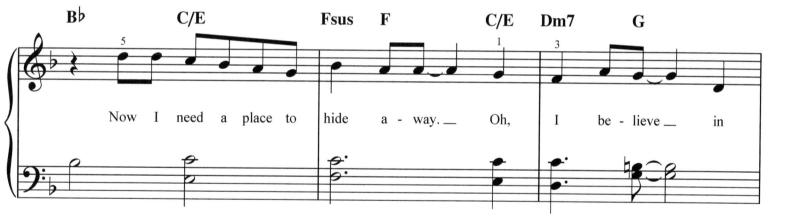

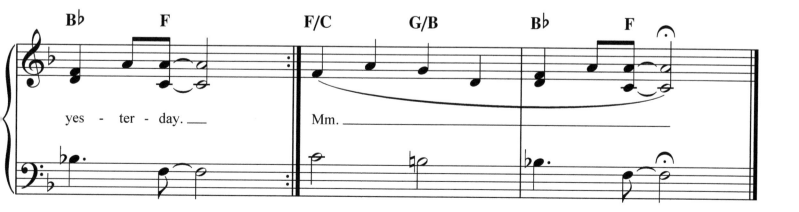

YOUR SONG

featured in the Motion Picture ROCKETMAN

Words and Music by ELTON JOHN
and BERNIE TAUPIN

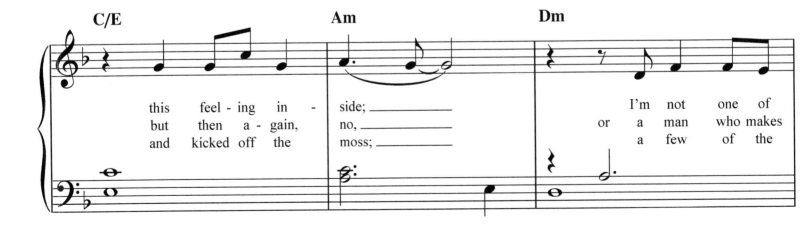

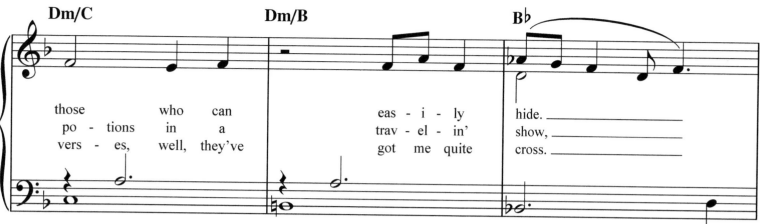

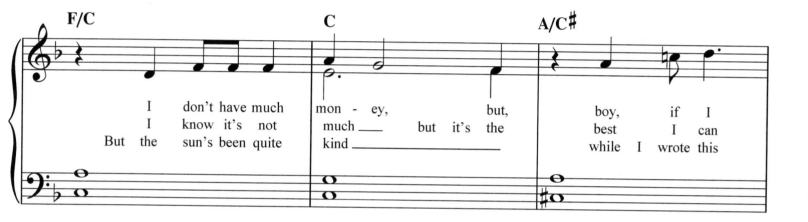

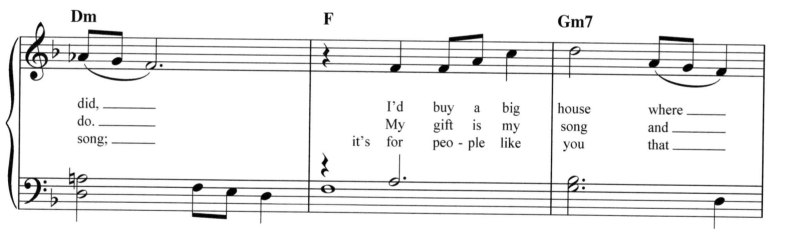

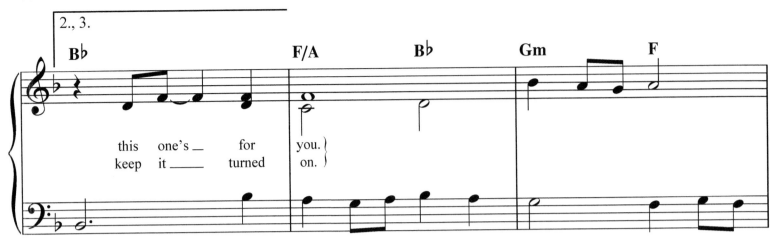

this one's ___ for you.
keep it ___ turned on.

And you can tell ev - 'ry - bod - y this is your

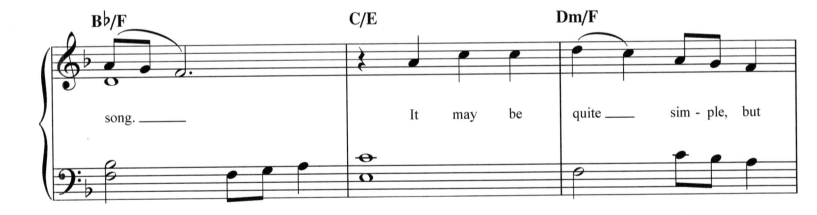

song. ___ It may be quite ___ sim - ple, but

To Coda ⊕

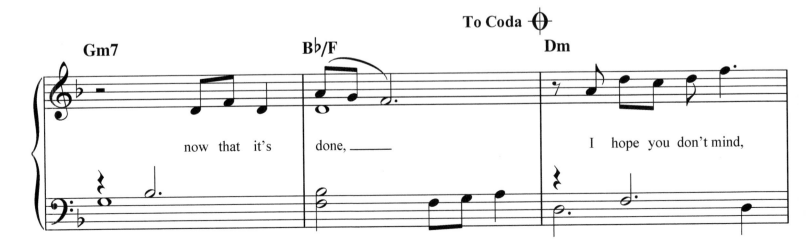

now that it's done, ___ I hope you don't mind,

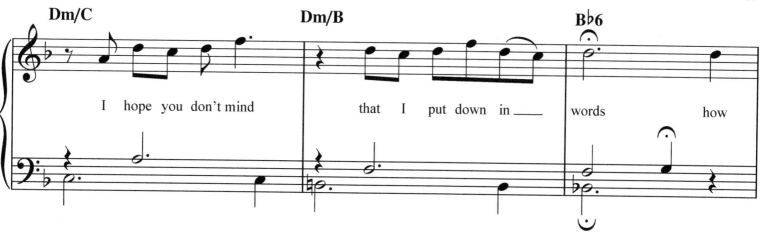

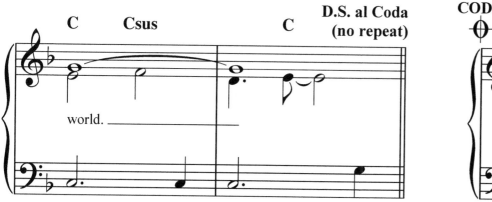

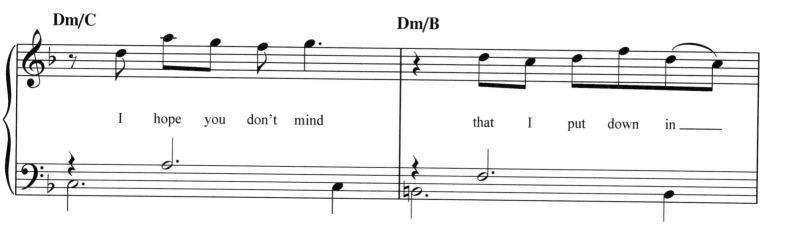

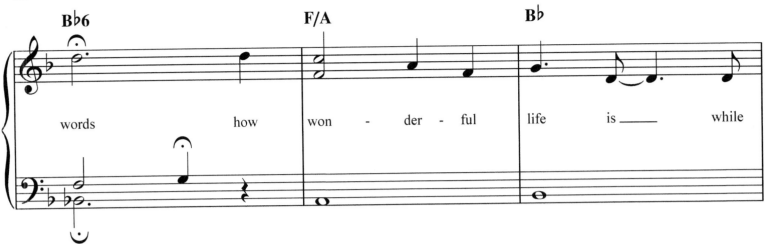

B♭6   **F/A**   **B♭**

words   how   won - der - ful   life   is ____ while

F   **B♭**

you're _   in   the   world.

F   **B♭/F**   **C/F**

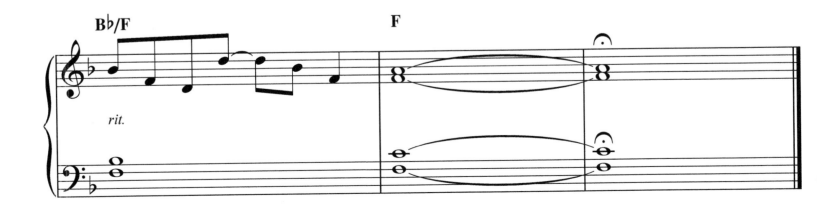

B♭/F   **F**

rit.

ZERO
from RALPH BREAKS THE INTERNET

Words and Music by DAN REYNOLDS,
WAYNE SERMON, BEN McKEE,
DANIEL PLATZMAN and JOHN HILL

With energy, in 2

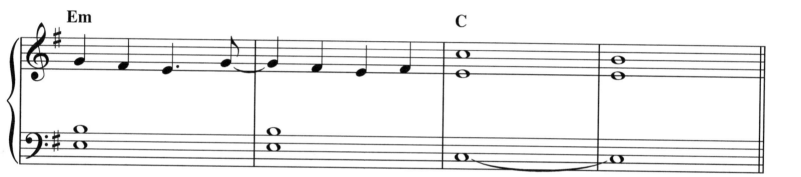

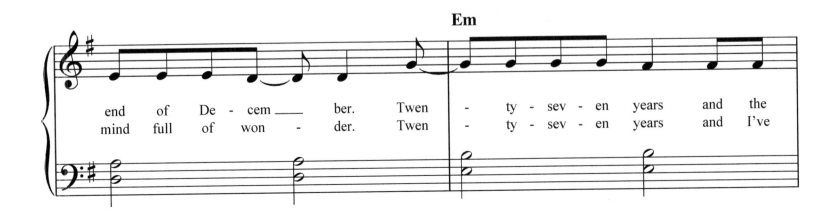

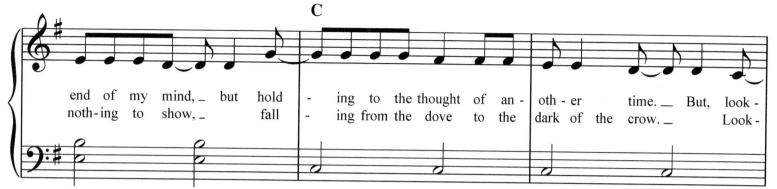

end of my mind, _ but hold - ing to the thought of an - oth - er time. _ But, look -
noth - ing to show, _ fall - ing from the dove to the dark of the crow. _ Look -

- ing to the ways of the ones be - fore _ me, look - ing for the path of the
- ing to the ways of the ones be - fore _ me, look - ing for the path of the

young and lone - ly. I _____ don't wan - na hear a - bout what to do. ___ I ___
young and lone - ly. I _____ don't wan - na hear a - bout what to do, ___ no. I ___

___ don't wan - na do it just to do it for you. ___
___ don't wan - na do it just to do it for you. ___

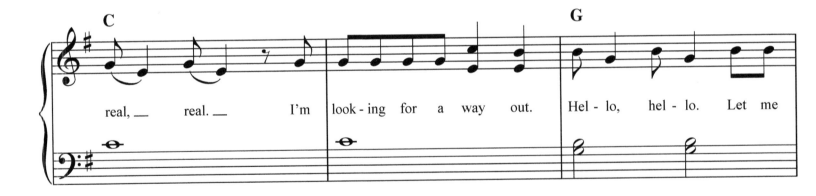

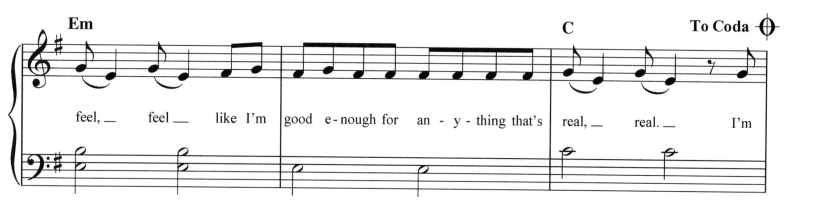

feel, __ feel __ like I'm good e-nough for an - y - thing that's real, __ real. __ I'm

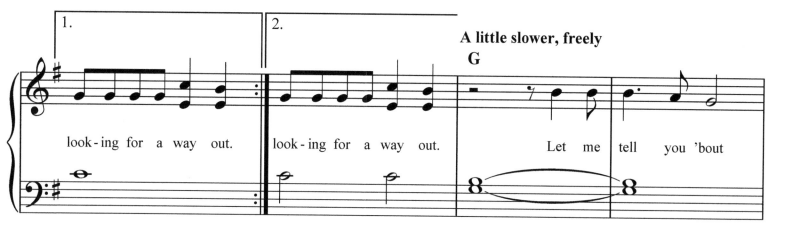

1.
look - ing for a way out.

2.
look - ing for a way out.

A little slower, freely

Let me tell you 'bout

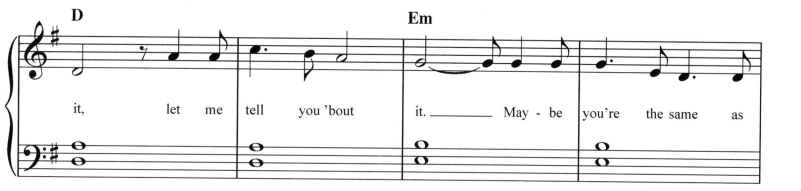

it, let me tell you 'bout it. _____ May - be you're the same as

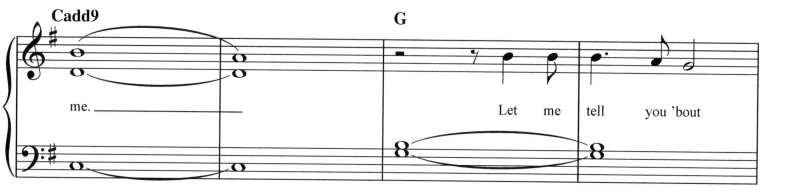

me. _____

Let me tell you 'bout

it,   let me tell   you 'bout   it.   They   say   that

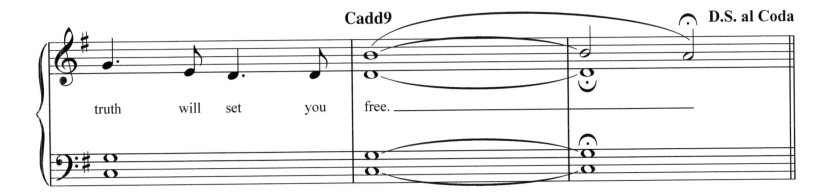

truth   will set   you   free. _____

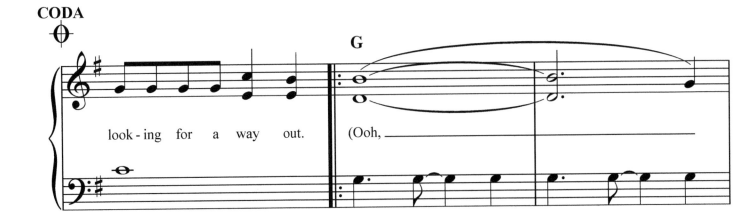

look-ing for a way out.   (Ooh, _____

ooh, _____   ooh, _____

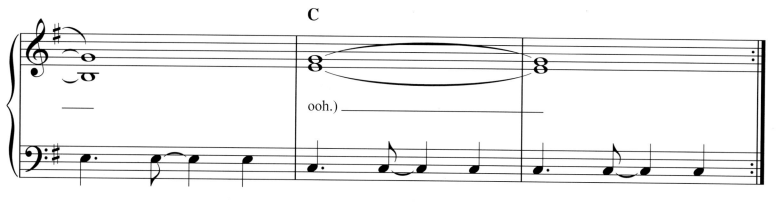

ooh.)

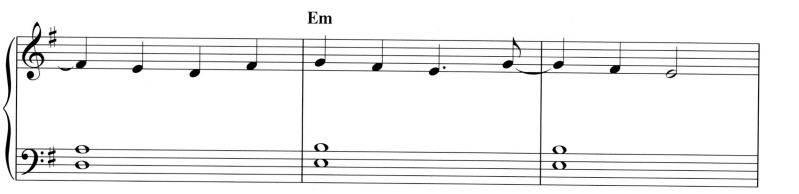

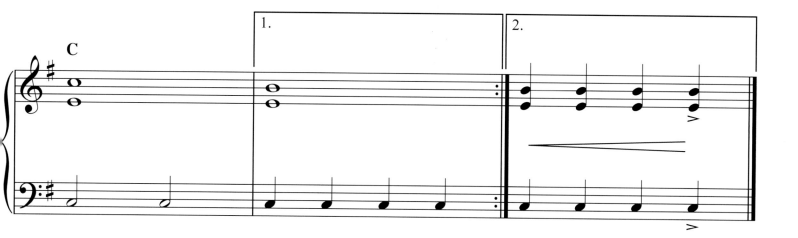

It's Easy to Play Your Favorite Songs with Hal Leonard Easy Piano Books

The Best Praise & Worship Songs Ever

The name says it all: over 70 of the best P&W songs today. Titles include: Awesome God • Blessed Be Your Name • Come, Now Is the Time to Worship • Days of Elijah • Here I Am to Worship • Open the Eyes of My Heart • Shout to the Lord • We Fall Down • and more.
00311312 ....$19.99

First 50 Popular Songs You Should Play on the Piano

50 great pop classics for beginning pianists to learn, including: Candle in the Wind • Chopsticks • Don't Know Why • Hallelujah • Happy Birthday to You • Heart and Soul • I Walk the Line • Just the Way You Are • Let It Be • Let It Go • Over the Rainbow • Piano Man • and many more.
00131140 ....$16.99

The Greatest Video Game Music

28 easy piano selections for the music that envelops you as you lose yourself in the world of video games, including: Angry Birds Theme • Assassin's Creed Revelations • Dragonborn (Skyrim Theme) • Elder Scrolls: Oblivion • Minecraft: Sweden • Rage of Sparta from God of War III • and more.
00202545 ....$17.99

Jumbo Easy Piano Songbook

200 classical favorites, folk songs and jazz standards. Includes: Amazing Grace • Beale Street Blues • Bridal Chorus • Buffalo Gals • Canon in D • Cielito Lindo • Danny Boy • The Entertainer • Für Elise • Greensleeves • Jamaica Farewell • Marianne • Molly Malone • Ode to Joy • Peg O' My Heart • Rockin' Robin • Yankee Doodle • dozens more!
00311014 ....$19.99

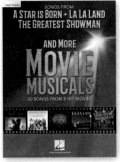

Songs from *A Star Is Born*, *The Greatest Showman*, *La La Land*, and More Movie Musicals

Movie musical lovers will delight in this songbook chock full of top-notch songs arranged for easy piano with lyrics from blockbuster movies. Includes: City of Stars from *La La Land* • Suddenly from *Les Misérables* • This Is Me from *The Greatest Showman* • Shallow from *A Star Is Born* • and more.
00287577 ....$17.99

50 Easy Classical Themes

Easy arrangements of 50 classical tunes representing more than 30 composers, including: Bach, Beethoven, Chopin, Debussy, Dvorak, Handel, Haydn, Liszt, Mozart, Mussorgsky, Puccini, Rossini, Schubert, Strauss, Tchaikovsky, Vivaldi, and more.
00311215 ....$14.99

Pop Songs for Kids

Kids from all corners of the world love and sing along to the songs of Taylor Swift, One Direction, Katy Perry, and other pop stars. This collection features 25 songs from these and many more artists in easy piano format. Includes: Brave • Can't Stop the Feeling • Firework • Home • Let It Go • Shake It Off • What Makes You Beautiful • and more.
00221920 ....$14.99

Simple Songs – The Easiest Easy Piano Songs

Play 50 of your favorite songs in the easiest of arrangements! Songs include: Castle on a Cloud • Do-Re-Mi • Happy Birthday to You • Hey Jude • Let It Go • Linus and Lucy • Over the Rainbow • Smile • Star Wars (Main Theme) • Tomorrow • and more.
00142041 ....$14.99

VH1's 100 Greatest Songs of Rock and Roll

The results from the VH1 show that featured the 100 greatest rock and roll songs of all time are here in this awesome collection! Songs include: Born to Run • Good Vibrations • Hey Jude • Hotel California • Imagine • Light My Fire • Like a Rolling Stone • Respect • and more.
00311110 ....$29.99

River Flows in You and Other Eloquent Songs for Easy Piano Solo

24 piano favorites arranged so that even beginning players can sound great. Includes: All of Me • Bella's Lullaby • Cristofori's Dream • Il Postino (The Postman) • Jessica's Theme (Breaking in the Colt) • The John Dunbar Theme • and more.
00137581 ....$14.99

Disney's My First Song Book

16 favorite songs to sing and play. Every page is beautifully illustrated with full-color art from Disney features. Songs include: Beauty and the Beast • Bibbidi-Bobbidi-Boo • Circle of Life • Cruella De Vil • A Dream Is a Wish Your Heart Makes • Hakuna Matata • Under the Sea • Winnie the Pooh • You've Got a Friend in Me • and more.
00310322 ....$17.99

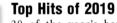

Top Hits of 2019

20 of the year's best are included in this collection arranged for easy piano with lyrics. Includes: Bad Guy (Billie Eilish) • I Don't Care (Ed Sheeran & Justin Bieber) • ME! (Taylor Swift feat. Brendon Urie) • Old Town Road (Remix) (Lil Nas X feat. Billy Ray Cyrus) • Senorita (Shawn Mendes & Camila Cabello) • Someone You Loved (Lewis Capaldi) • and more.
00302273 ....$16.99

Get complete song lists and more at
www.halleonard.com

Prices, contents, and availability subject to change without notice
Disney characters and artwork © Disney Enterprises, Inc.